Discover Sydenham and Catford

Discover
SYDENHAM
and
CATFORD

A comprehensive guide to SYDENHAM,
CRYSTAL PALACE, FOREST HILL,
CATFORD, HITHER GREEN & GROVE PARK

by DARRELL SPURGEON

GREENWICH GUIDE-BOOKS

Copyright © Darrell Spurgeon 1999

All rights reserved. No part of this book may be copied or otherwise reproduced, stored in a retrieval system, or transmitted, in any form or by any means, electronic, mechanical, photocopying, recording or otherwise, without the prior permission of the author.

First published in Great Britain 1999 by
Greenwich Guide-Books,
72 Kidbrooke Grove, Blackheath, London SE3 0LG
(phone 0181-858 5831)

Other volumes in the same series by the same author:
Volume I (first edition), covering Woolwich, Plumstead, Shooters Hill, East Wickham, Abbey Wood & Thamesmead (published 1990, out of print)
Volume II, covering Greenwich, Westcombe & Charlton (published 1991, out of print)
Volume III, covering Eltham, New Eltham, Mottingham, Grove Park, Kidbrooke & Shooters Hill (published 1992, out of print)
Volume IV, covering Bexley, Bexleyheath, Welling, Sidcup, Footscray & North Cray (published 1993)
Volume V, covering Crayford, Slade Green, Erith, Belvedere, Abbey Wood & Thamesmead (published 1995)
Volume VI (new edition of Volume I), covering Woolwich, The Royal Arsenal, Woolwich Common, Plumstead, Shooters Hill & Abbey Wood (published 1996)
Volume VII, covering Deptford, New Cross, Brockley, Lewisham & Ladywell (published 1997)

Front cover photograph is Horniman Museum (Harrison Townsend 1901)
gazetteer reference - Forest Hill 19

Printed in Great Britain by Short Run Press, Exeter

A catalogue record for this book is available from the British Library
ISBN 0 9515624 7 9

CONTENTS

Foreword   page 6

SYDENHAM
Introduction   9
Section 'A' (Lower Sydenham & Bell Green)   13
Section 'B' (Westwood Hill & Lawrie Park)   17
Section 'C' (Sydenham Hill & Wells Park)   23
Section 'D' (Kirkdale & Sydenham Park)   27
Suggested Walks   32

CRYSTAL PALACE
Introduction   35
Section 'A' (Crystal Palace Park)   39
Section 'B' (The Fringes of the Park)   43

FOREST HILL
Introduction   46
Section 'A' (Honor Oak)   49
Section 'B' (Horniman Museum & Gardens)   54
Section 'C' (The Railway Suburb)   57
Suggested Walks   62

CATFORD
Introduction   64
Section 'A' (Town Centre & Rushey Green)   67
Section 'B' (Blythe Hill & Perry Hill)   71
Section 'C' (Southend, Bellingham & Downham)   75
Suggested Walk   79

HITHER GREEN
Introduction   80
Gazetteer   81

GROVE PARK
Introduction   86
Gazetteer   87

Notes on some Architects & Artists   90
Bibliography   92
Index   93

MAPS
Sydenham Section 'A'   12
Sydenham Sections 'B', 'C' & 'D'   18
Crystal Palace general map   38
Forest Hill general map   48
Catford Sections 'A' & 'B'   66
Catford Section 'C'   74
Hither Green map   82
Grove Park map   88

FOREWORD

This book covers six areas - Sydenham, Crystal Palace, Forest Hill, Catford, Hither Green and Grove Park.

These areas are mostly in the London Borough of Lewisham. The exceptions are that part of Sydenham to the west of Sydenham Hill and that part of Forest Hill to the north of Honor Oak Park, which are in the London Borough of Southwark; Crystal Palace Park and the southern part of the Lawrie Park Estate, Sydenham, which are in the London Borough of Bromley; and the fringes of Crystal Palace Park, which present a confusing picture, as they are variously in the London Boroughs of Southwark, Bromley, Lambeth and Croydon as well as Lewisham.

The London Borough of Lewisham was created in 1965 by the merger of the Metropolitan Boroughs of Deptford and Lewisham, which had been set up in 1900. Before 1965, the areas now in Southwark were in the Metropolitan Borough of Camberwell; Crystal Palace Park in the Urban District of Penge; and the southern part of the Lawrie Park Estate, Sydenham, in the Municipal Borough of Beckenham. The areas in Lewisham were all in the Metropolitan Borough of Lewisham.

The basic framework for each of the six areas consists of a brief introduction, gazetteer, map(s), and (in Sydenham, Forest Hill and Catford) suggested walk(s). Each location in the gazetteers is identified (using location numbers) on a map. There are suggested walks where places of interest are concentrated within an area which makes walking practicable and interesting, and where guidance would be helpful.

Sydenham is divided into four sections - Section 'A' Lower Sydenham & Bell Green; Section 'B' Westwood Hill & Lawrie Park; Section 'C' Sydenham Hill & Wells Park; and Section 'D' Kirkdale & Sydenham Park. There are two maps, one covering Section 'A' and the other covering Sections 'A', 'B' and 'C'. There are suggested walks which cover most locations in each section.

Crystal Palace is divided into two sections - Section 'A' Crystal Palace Park; and Section 'B' The Fringes of the Park. One map covers both sections. There is no suggested walk, as the sequence of locations in the gazetteers makes it easy to work out suitable walks.

Forest Hill is divided into three sections - Section 'A' Honor Oak; Section 'B' Horniman Museum & Gardens; and Section 'C' The Railway Suburb. One map covers all sections. The suggested walks cover most locations in Section 'A', and many locations in Section 'C' (others are not included, to avoid making the walk too long); Section 'B' is not covered, as the gazetteer entry for the Horniman Museum & Gardens indicates clearly how best to see the places of interest.

Catford is divided into three sections - Section 'A' Town Centre & Rushey Green; Section 'B' Blythe Hill & Perry Hill; and Section 'C' Southend, Bellingham & Downham. There are two maps, one covering Sections 'A' and 'B', and the other Section 'C'. The suggested walk covers most locations in Sections 'A' and 'B'. There is no suggested walk for Section 'C', as the locations are not numerous and cover quite a large area.

Hither Green and Grove Park are not divided into sections. Each area has a map. There are no suggested walks - in Hither Green the locations are spread over a large area, and in Grove Park the locations are not numerous.

Although the introductions to the areas contain some historical background, and certain locations have some historical information in indented paragraphs, the guide makes no pretensions to be a work of local history. Again, although some non-specialist knowledge of architecture is assumed, the guide does not become involved in detailed architectural analysis, and a conscious attempt has been made to avoid architectural jargon. Readers interested in further information on local history and architectural detail may like to consult the list of books at the end of the guide.

The gazetteers are intended as a comprehensive list of buildings and landscape features which are of visual interest, though the choice of places is inevitably very personal. The emphasis is on what is there now, not so much on what has been there in the past, and practical information is given on how best to see each place. The starring system in the gazetteers, with stars being given to the most outstanding locations, is intended to help visitors to allocate their time to the best advantage.

The maps, which are the key to the guide, adopt the same practical approach. Nearly every place mentioned in the text is pinpointed on a map in such a way as to make it easy to find and notice. The maps are indicative and not to scale, and only show those roads which are likely to be important to the visitor. It is suggested that a proper and more detailed road map of the area be obtained.

When using the Gazetteer and following the suggested walks, it is advisable always to try to have a clear idea of the direction you are facing, ie north, south, east or west.

Italics are used for information on access, for other practical advice, for introductory notes before the walks, and also for cross-referencing. Paragraphs with information of a specifically historical nature are indented.

The sequence of locations in the gazetteers broadly follows the order in the suggested walks, and locations not included in the walks are slotted into the sequence in a way which would make it more convenient for a visit. For sections without a suggested walk, the sequence of locations follows a broadly circular pattern.

Some locations are difficult of access, and the guide gives practical information on how to overcome this difficulty. In some cases this may not always be possible, but it is certainly worth trying. In other cases, a certain initiative is demanded; for example, it is usually necessary to phone or call at the clergyman's residence to obtain access to church interiors. In my experience most clergymen are extremely helpful in facilitating this. And many places which are private will not in practice turn away the interested visitor asking permission to view. The text includes contact telephone numbers and/or addresses which may be found helpful in this context.

8 - FOREWORD

Of the publications which I have consulted, I wish to make particular mention of 'London 2: South', by Bridget Cherry and Nikolaus Pevsner, in the Penguin Buildings of England series; the Department of the Environment List of Buildings of Architectural & Historic Interest, which can be consulted at the National Monuments Record (London office), 55 Blandford Street, London W1; 'Lewisham, History & Guide', by John Coulter; 'The Palace of the People', by Graham Reeves; 'Hither Green, the Forgotten Hamlet', by Godfrey Smith (this book is the source of most of the factual material in the Hither Green section); and several publications of Ken White. These and other publications which I have found useful are listed in the bibliography at the end.

I wish to give very special thanks and acknowledgment to numerous local people who helped me in various ways.

In my previous book, which covered Deptford and Lewisham, I acknowledged fully the invaluable help given me by John Coulter, of the Local Studies Centre at Lewisham Library, Lewisham High Street. I would say that this time his help has been even more generous. The book has been enriched by the factual detail he has supplied, often from research he has undertaken on my behalf. I very much appreciate his interest and involvement, and the amount of time he has devoted to me.

Jean Wait, the Borough Archivist at the Local Studies Centre, also dealt courteously and efficiently with my many requests for information. Both Jean and John read the draft text in full; Steve Grindlay, archivist of the Sydenham Society, read the text on Sydenham, Crystal Palace and Forest Hill; Melvyn Harrison, of the Crystal Palace Foundation, the text on Crystal Palace; Godfrey Smith the text on Catford and Hither Green; John King (of the Lewisham Local History Society) the text on Grove Park; and Kenneth Richardson the text on Grove Park and on the Sir Charles Nicholson churches. All offered many useful suggestions and much constructive criticism.

Many thanks also to Philip Ashford, of Lewisham Planning; Ken White; Jennifer Beever, of Horniman Museum; Gillian Heywood, for showing me around Sydenham High School; Len Reilly; Harold Hamilton; Phil Chambers, of Southwark Planning; David Allkins, of Thames Water; Jon Broome, of Architype, for information on self-build; Douglas Earle, for information on Hither Green Hospital.

Many thanks also to Jim Pope for invaluable advice on production and design; and to Roy Atterbury for much good advice, and for expert processing of the photographs.

The area covered by this guide, like any urban area, is subject to the process of change, and the situation with regard to the condition and function (or even the existence) of buildings, their accessibility etc can change quite rapidly. However, the information was checked before going to print, and if anyone is misled in any way, I can only offer my apologies.

Darrell Spurgeon,
Blackheath, May 1999

SYDENHAM

Introduction

Sydenham falls naturally into two parts, divided by the railway to Croydon and Brighton - Lower Sydenham to the east, and Upper Sydenham to the west. At the start of the 19th century there was a rural village in Lower Sydenham and hilly heathland in Upper Sydenham. Over a period of just over 50 years three events transformed Sydenham into a suburb - the enclosure of Sydenham Common 1810-19; the construction of the railway to Croydon 1836-39, largely following the route of the Croydon Canal, which had been completed in 1809; and the opening of the Crystal Palace in 1854.

But Sydenham does not have the atmosphere of an ordinary suburb. Upper Sydenham retains a rural atmosphere, with many large houses surviving in wide streets; it climbs up to the ridge, over 100 metres high, of Sydenham Hill, and there are wonderful views from many points in its hilly streets. Lower Sydenham is low-lying and more densely built up, but this was the original village, and Sydenham Road, which was the original village street, preserves buildings which are the oldest in the whole area.

Early Sydenham

Sydenham was originally part of the manor of Lewisham. In the medieval period, Place House, which was located near the present junction of Catford Hill and Perry Hill, came to be considered the manor house of Sydenham, though the area is nowadays more often considered part of Catford. Development then spread along Perry Hill to Bell Green, then known as Sydenham Green. Of this very early development, nothing now remains.

From Bell Green by the mid 18th century a ribbon of buildings extended westwards forming a hamlet along the present Sydenham Road.

Where Sydenham Road now ends, the ground rises quite steeply, to the west and to the north, up to the ridge called Sydenham Hill. This was Westwood Common, later called Sydenham Common, and beyond the ridge was the Great North Wood. It was not until after the Common was enclosed 1810-19 that the area was developed and became known as Upper Sydenham. Before enclosure Upper Sydenham was hardly populated, apart from a few houses around the Greyhound pub, Peak Hill and the lower part of Westwood Hill (the only survivor being, in part, Old Cedars), and a cluster of buildings around Sydenham Wells.

Sydenham Wells

The mineral springs reputed to have medicinal qualities were first discovered on Westwood Common in the 1640s; they became a very popular place to visit, though their popularity began to decline after the enclosure, and they were not used after the 1830s. There were several wells, the site of the main well being by the present junction of Wells Park Road and Taylors Lane; the present ponds in Sydenham Wells Park are fed from the same springs.

Later other spas were developed in this part of South East London - Dulwich Wells, at the junction of Lordship Lane and Dulwich Common, from 1739; and more famous, Beulah Spa, in Upper Norwood, from 1831, but lasting only till 1855.

In the early 19th century

In 1809 the Croydon Canal had reached the eastern edge of Sydenham Common; it linked Croydon to the Grand Surrey Canal at New Cross, then on to the Surrey Docks and the Thames. It was not very successful and did not in itself have much of an impact on Sydenham, but in 1836 it was acquired by the London & Croydon Railway, which used the canal bed broadly as a route for the construction of the new railway line from London Bridge to West Croydon which opened in 1839. Sydenham Station was on the route, and this had a massive impact on the Sydenham area.

But before this happened, Sydenham Common had been enclosed. There was an attempt, 200 years previously, to enclose the Common, but this had been foiled by Abraham Colfe, the Vicar of Lewisham; he led a deputation to James I of small farmers, who had used the Common for grazing. But in 1810 the Lewisham Enclosure Act was passed.

Development was initially slower than might have been expected. A number of cottages soon appeared in and around Kirkdale and Dartmouth Road, of which weatherboarded pairs have survived in Kirkdale, Mount Gardens and Taylors Lane, followed by some larger houses around Kirkdale and along Sydenham Hill. But there were enough new residents to justify the building of the large new church of St Bartholomews, which opened in 1832.

However, the major consequence of enclosure was to facilitate later development, first following the opening of Sydenham Station (this included the attractive Sydenham Park Estate, occupying the site of a reservoir for the canal); then, most important of all, the arrival of the Crystal Palace in 1854.

The Crystal Palace, and its impact

It is difficult now to envisage the impact the Crystal Palace had on London, and in particular South London - it was the greatest leisure attraction the country had ever known. It is difficult also to exaggerate the extent to which it transformed Sydenham. The Crystal Palace was not strictly part of Sydenham, rather part of Penge, but it continued the ridge of Sydenham Hill westwards and loomed at the top of the approach up Westwood Hill. An explosion in the population of Sydenham was inevitable. New developments started even in 1852, when the building of the Crystal Palace commenced, two years before it was completed.

Grand mansions were built along Sydenham Hill and Crescent Wood Road, also in and around Westwood Hill. Large (but not quite so grand) houses were built in and around Kirkdale, in the gaps on Westwood Hill, and in side roads like Jew's Walk. By the 1880s the building of such large houses was coming to an end, though two great mansions were built in Sydenham Hill as late as 1898. Many of these houses have of course gone, but surprisingly many have survived.

The Lawrie Park Estate

Perhaps the most interesting of the new developments was the Lawrie Park Estate, to the south of Westwood Hill. It was developed after George Wythes (a developer who later filled up the space between Chislehurst and Bromley with the great houses of Bickley) acquired the area from the Lawrie family, who had formerly occupied two large old houses on the Estate - Sydenham Hall and Westwood House. The Lawrie Park Estate comprised a number of large houses in very large grounds along a few spaciously laid out streets, one of which (celebrated in a painting of Pissarro) is of outstanding appeal - Lawrie Park Avenue. The development here, and in Lawrie Park Road, Border Road, Lawrie Park Crescent and Lawrie Park Gardens was largely complete by 1870. Many of these houses have survived, but it has to be said that the quality of their design does not generally measure up to the high standard of the road layout and environment.

The Edwardian period

The impact of the Crystal Palace on Lower Sydenham was inevitably less dramatic. Here, a greater influence had been the expansion of the gas industry at Bell Green from 1853.

Sydenham Road in Lower Sydenham is now the main shopping centre of Sydenham. However, before 1900 the centre had been around the junction of Kirkdale and Dartmouth Road, and in fact the parts of these streets by the junction were then known as High Street. But the construction of Grand Parade in Sydenham Road c1900 and the enlargement of Cobb's department store near the station in 1902 served to shift the main shopping focus away to Lower Sydenham. Any remaining gaps in the pattern of streets off Sydenham Road soon filled with Edwardian style housing; the prevailing style of these streets, including those developed shortly beforehand, is Edwardian. Much of this Edwardian housing is in fact very appealing, particularly the Thorpe Estate and the district around Newlands Park.

Sydenham now

Around the end of the century the Crystal Palace was beginning to lose its appeal. It was not a commercial success, at least partly because it was not allowed to open on Sundays. It was put up for sale in 1911, and bought for the nation in 1913. But it never recovered its former glory, and the story ended with the disastrous fire of 1936.

It could be said that Sydenham mirrored the fortunes of the Crystal Palace. It ceased to be quite such a fashionable suburb as these fortunes began to wane. But Sydenham retains many fine houses in rural and hilly environs, and there are hidden pockets of delight which remain largely unknown.

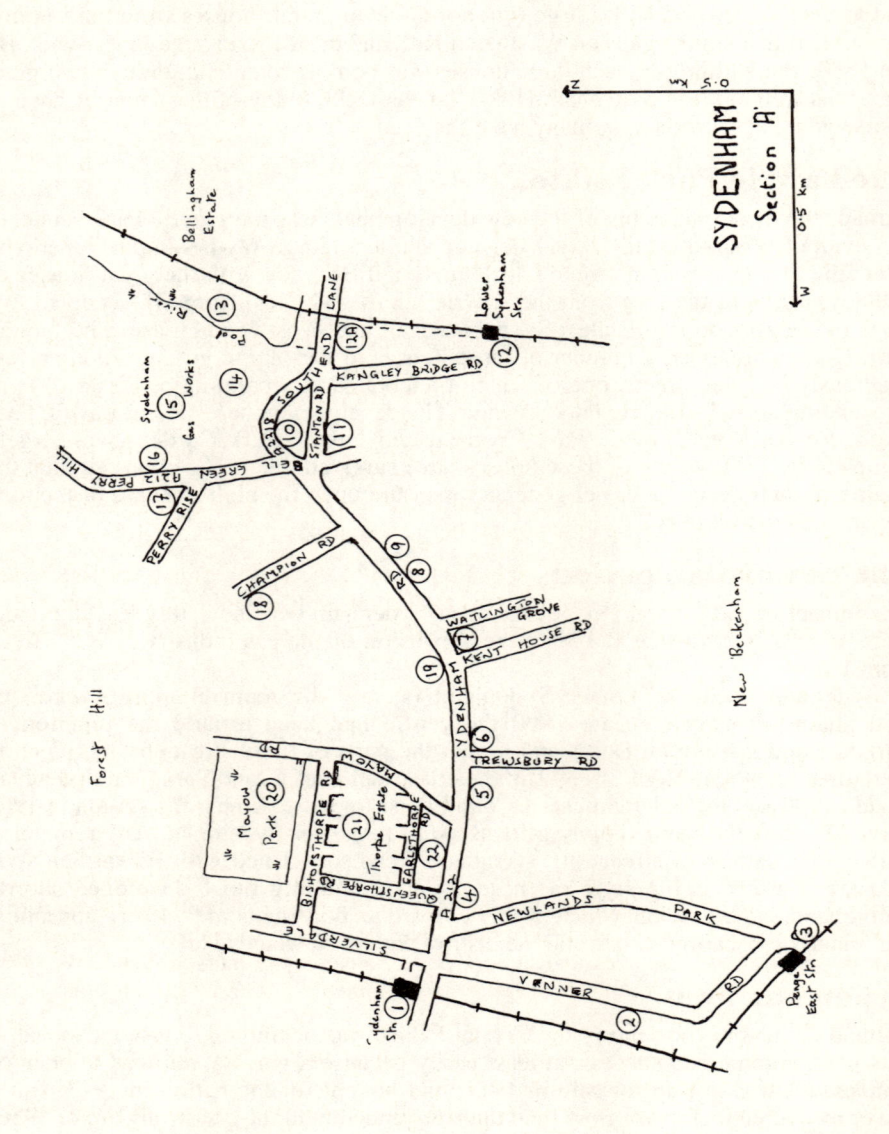

SYDENHAM
Section 'A'

SYDENHAM

Gazetteer

Section 'A' LOWER SYDENHAM & BELL GREEN

1. Sydenham Station was opened in 1839 by the London & Croydon Railway, using the bed of the disused Croydon Canal. The original station building was on the south side of the road bridge, its location now a blank wall between the bridge and a telephone kiosk. A separate 'down' side building to the north of the road bridge was opened in 1875, and this building (now the only entrance to the station) survives in Sydenham Station Approach. The original building (largely rebuilt in 1856) was demolished in 1982, though traces of the old 'up' side platform can still be seen to the south of the road bridge. The new 'up' side platform, accessible by a new footbridge from the 'down' side, was erected about 100 metres north in 1982.

2. 88 Venner Road. An impressive classical villa of the 1880s, rather startling in this street full of Edwardian style houses. It is rusticated, and has intricate cast iron work - note the railing along the parapet and the slender twisted columns of the full width loggia.

3. Penge East Station retains its original Gothic building of 1863 on the south side - two projecting end pavilions with a lower recessed section between them. The platforms are linked by an old bridge; note also the old level-crossing keeper's cottage jutting onto the south side platform. It was opened as Penge Lane Station 1863, and renamed Penge East 1923. From here the 'up' line goes through the Penge Tunnel (two kilometres long) to Sydenham Hill Station *(see Sydenham 61).*

4. *32/34 Sydenham Road, called Priory Cottage and Woodmans Cottage respectively, are an interesting and attractive pair of semi-detached houses, early 18th century (perhaps as early as c1700), the oldest houses in Sydenham and among the oldest semi-detached houses in London. Both houses have half-gables above doors with Gibbs surrounds, weatherboarded sides, and mansard roofs with dormers. No 34 is difficult to see behind the fencing.

5. Golden Lion, 116 Sydenham Road, a fine early 19th century classical pub. There has been a pub on the site since at least 1740.

Over the top of the shops on the opposite side of the road a large house of 1806 is visible. Formerly called Clune House, it looks in poor condition.

6. All Saints Church, Trewsbury Road. Only the ugly west end of this clearly unfinished church by George Fellowes Prynne of 1903 can be seen from Trewsbury

Road. The east end cannot really be seen at all, as it is concealed by later buildings. There is an unsatisfactory view of the top of the church from Sydenham Road.

But the *****interior** *(contact 0181-778 3065)* is of outstanding appeal and interest. It is of brick, very lofty and severe, and is dominated by the great chancel arch, with its stone screen built right up to the top. Very tall octagonal brick piers along the high arcades, tall narrow windows in the chancel and aisles, wooden barrel roof. However, only three bays of the nave were built, and the west end, even in the interior, is poor.

Next to the church are the present church hall, brick, of 1933; and, on the corner of the main road, the old and derelict *****All Saints Hall**, a small Gothic chapel with narrow Gothic windows.

> Its date is uncertain, basically and in part it may be c1760 or possibly slightly earlier; it occupies the site of a Dissenters' meeting house which is on John Rocque's map of 1744. It became an Anglican chapel of ease in 1795, when major rebuilding took place and it became known as Christ Church. Apart from a brief period as a non-conformist chapel 1867-73, it remained Christ Church until 1903, when the present All Saints Church *(see above)* was built and it became All Saints Hall.

The last major rebuild was in 1845, when the north entrance with its steeple was added; there is now just a truncated tower, the spire having since been removed. There is a proposal to convert the old chapel for housing.

120/124 Sydenham Road, next to the old chapel, are plain Georgian brick houses c1800; no 120 has an altered ground floor, nos 122/124 was formerly one house.

7. The Prince Alfred, 178 Sydenham Road, is a pleasant pub c1865. Just to the east is **Watlington Grove**, with terraces of cottages of the late 1860s facing each other.

8. Church of Our Lady & St Philip Neri, Sydenham Road, a Roman Catholic brick church of 1958, designed by Walters & Kerr Bate. Behind a great square bell-tower (added 1961) against the road is the church, with a smaller tower over the crossing. Note the wavy stone pattern all around the doorcases of both church and tower.

The **interior** *(call at the presbytery next door)* is distinguished by the large crossing, which has four great semi-circular concrete arches which intersect at each corner to provide four enclosed spaces, in three cases occupied by small chapels. It is otherwise unremarkable, though note the window in the south transept with stained glass by Goddard & Gibbs showing the death of St Philip Neri.

The **presbytery**, 208 Sydenham Road, is an intriguing mock-Tudor building, half-timbered and vivid white, a stark contrast to the church; it is of 1929, so was built for the earlier church of 1882, which was further west. A great gable above the entrance sweeps through the upper floor and into the roof, incorporating a two-storey oriel.

At the rear to the left is a small extension, which was actually a late 19th century extension to an early 18th century house which was the presbytery from 1919 to 1929, when it was demolished for the new building. Sir George Grove, the writer on music, lived in the former house 1860-1900, and this is commemorated by a Lewisham Council plaque on the front wall.

> Sir George Grove (1820-1900), was the founder and editor of 'Grove's Dictionary of Music and Musicians', which continues to flourish, and founder of the Royal College of Music. He was the first Secretary of the Crystal Palace Company, which was responsible for transferring the Crystal Palace from Hyde Park to its Sydenham site *(see Crystal Palace Introduction)*. Together with the conductor August Manns, Grove promoted a series of outstanding and remarkable musical performances at the Palace. Before moving to this site in 1860, he lived at 14 Westwood Hill *(see Sydenham 26)* from 1852. Grove was buried at Ladywell Cemetery.

9. *Sydenham Library, a striking baroque building of 1904, red brick with lots of stone dressings. The original entrance was in a porch facing Sydenham Road, flanked by the surviving double Ionic columns; under the gables on either side are Venetian windows with oval cartouches below. More Venetian windows are along the side to the present entrance, built when the porch was removed in 1973. Attractive interior with arcades and three domes for top-lighting.

10. The Bell, 59 Bell Green, on the traffic island, a classical pub c1845; a lower extension to the left was added later.

Next door is **The Old Bath House**, 65 Bell Green, opened as Lewisham Public Baths 1907, with a tiled ground floor and red brick upper floor, now an architectural salvage yard.

11. Haseltine School, an enormous London School Board block of 1885, with gabled dormers; though very regular, it lacks harmony.

12. Lower Sydenham Station, on the Mid Kent Line, the present building being the third station, c1992. The first station was opened nearer to Southend Lane in 1857; the second station was opened on this site in 1906.

It is accessible from Southend Lane by a road and footpath alongside **Railway Tavern (12A)**, 401 Southend Lane, a pub c1867.

13. *Pool River Walk. This parkland riverside walkway, 700 metres long, from Bell Green to Bellingham, was designed by Symonds Travers Morgan 1996. Formerly, this section of the River Pool bisected the gasworks site in an underground culvert; it was relocated in the open along a meandering route to the east of the site, between Savacentre and the Mid Kent Line embankment. Although the river is in a concrete channel, it looks attractive because of the landscaping and good design features throughout.

Starting from Southend Lane, the walk crosses a new bridge, then runs to the east of the river, swooping up and down, above and alongside the river edge. It then crosses a prominent blue tied-arch bridge, which marks the central point and gives access to Savacentre. From here, the walk runs to the west of the river, which ripples over stones and a series of weirs; after passing a reed-pool to the left, it reaches the end at Broadmead, where there is a basic modern bridge over the river and a bridge up and over the Mid-Kent Line into the Bellingham Estate. Beyond, the river has natural banks; the river and an older footpath continue northwards to the confluence of the river with the River Ravensbourne by Catford Hill *(see Catford 40A)*.

> The River Pool (also known in its upper parts as Chaffinch Brook) rises in Shirley, and flows through Elmers End and Cator Park, Beckenham, before reaching Sydenham.

14. Savacentre. This vast store of 1995, with its pervasive style, its blue and grey colours, dominates the area around. Great inverted beams, supported by high-tech pillars, mark the store entrance.

15. Sydenham Gas Works. Only two gas holders, of 1881 and 1890, remain. Savacentre and the Pool River Walk *(see above)* now occupy part of the old Gas Works site. The remainder of the site is derelict, and proposals for developing it have caused considerable local controversy.

> North Surrey Gas Company began production at Bell Green, though to the south of Southend Lane, in 1853; it became the Crystal Palace & District Gas Company in

1854. The Company had moved to this site, north of Southend Lane, by 1863. It changed its name to South Suburban Gas Company in 1904. The South Metropolitan Gas Company reached an agreement in 1927 with the South Suburban which was equivalent to an amalgamation. At its peak 2000 people were employed on the site and it was one of the largest gasworks in Britain. Gas production here ceased in 1969, but part of the site continued in use until the 1980s, and at present two gas holders remain out of four previously on the site. *(See also 16.)*

16. Livesey Memorial Hall. An interesting building of 1911, built for employees of South Suburban Gas Company as a memorial for Sir George Livesey. The double-arched porch is topped by a terracotta balustrade with urn-like finials on piers at each end. Between porch and balustrade is a faience panel with art nouveau lettering and floral stems on a green background. Note also the end bays with Venetian windows under gables. The interior has a large hall with classical pilasters around the walls, and a portrait of Livesey.

George Livesey was born in 1834, and was brought up alongside the Old Kent Road works of the South Metropolitan Gas Company. He started work there in 1848, and became Company Secretary & Engineer in 1871. He became Chair in 1881, by which time the Company had become the most powerful gas company in London, setting the price of gas. He soon became Chair of the adjacent Crystal Palace Gas Company, which changed its name to South Suburban Gas Company in 1904, with its centre at Bell Green. He introduced great technological changes into the gas industry, and was a pioneer of co-partnership (profit-sharing). He was knighted in 1904, died in 1908, and is buried in Nunhead Cemetery. *(See also 15.)*

In front of the Hall, to the right, is the **Livesey Hall War Memorial**, designed by Sydney March 1920, with plaques commemorating employees of the company who died in both world wars. The memorial has a life-size angel in bronze, standing on a ball entwined with serpents, with quite extraordinary detailing.

17. Church of God of Prophecy, a classical building of 1883, was originally Perry Hill Baptist Mission Hall; it became a Salvation Army hall in 1931.

18. St Michaels School, Champion Road. A substantial complex of 1871 designed by Edwin Nash, in a mix of Gothic and arts & crafts styles, with steep gables and very tall chimneys. The infant school to the north in Champion Crescent is of 1896.

Adjacent is the **Church of St Michael & All Angels**, an impressive long but simple brick building of 1958 by David Nye, with large gables at either end. Light and spacious interior. (Edwin Nash's church of 1864 was demolished following war damage; the school hall is now on the site.)

19. 215 Sydenham Road, a fine detached classical house c1870. Note the unusual classical features, particularly the porch with its strange capitals, and the dressings around the upper floor windows.

20. Mayow Park, a pleasant but rather featureless park, with some fine trees. It was opened in 1878, and this is commemorated by a fountain in the park.

21. Thorpe Estate. This Edwardian enclave between Bishopsthorpe Road and Earlsthorpe Road was built 1900-14. It has many stylish terraces, groups and pairs. Some houses, particularly along Queensthorpe Road, have pargetting in the gables.

22. 43/111 Sydenham Road, known as **Grand Parade** when built c1900 (nos 73/85 were replaced after war damage). These stately and impressive terraces dominate the shopping area.

SYDENHAM

Gazetteer

Section 'B' WESTWOOD HILL & LAWRIE PARK
(See map on page 18)

23. *The Greyhound, 315 Kirkdale, now called Fewterer & Firkin ('fewterer' means 'keeper of greyhounds' in Middle English). This is the oldest surviving inn of Sydenham, dating back to before 1726, but the present building (with its dramatic three gables) is a rebuild c1870. Note the small rounded oriels on either side of the front entrance. At the back is an appealing bar in a conservatory with Victorian tiled floor and tiled wall designs; this was the entrance to the Greyhound Hotel.

24. Cobb's Corner. This corner building, with its wonderful dome, was added in 1902 by Walter Cobb to his drapery shop, which had opened in 1860 in adjoining premises along Kirkdale.

25. *Church of St Bartholomew, Westwood Hill, a Gothic brick church of 1832 by Lewis Vulliamy. The chancel was added and the clerestory windows enlarged by Edwin Nash in 1858. The church is impressive, but it is also severe, with its castellated tower, nave, aisles and chancel giving it a fortress-like appearance. It is set in a small churchyard with many tombstones, and a lych-gate of 1906.

> The church originally acted as a chapel-of-ease to St Marys Lewisham, and did not become the parish church of Sydenham until 1856.
> Edwin Nash made a series of alterations in stages which transformed the interior of the church. In 1858 he added the apsidal chancel, raised the roof and enlarged the clerestory windows. In 1874 he clad the brick columns in stone, and added carved heads at the top. In 1883 he removed the west gallery, and widened the north aisle considerably (since 1986 it has been the church hall, cut off from the church).

The church is normally open between 0930 and 1130 on Saturday mornings. Otherwise contact 0181-778 5290 or 776 5722.

The *interior is quite spectacular, tall, wide and spacious, though the nave seems dark and sombre. The dominant features, on entering through the south porch, are the brilliant east window and the grand chancel arch.

The chancel is colourful and full of interest, though perhaps at odds with the nave. The reredos (of the Epiphany) and the flanking archangel panels, with their bold relief figures, are extraordinary, by Henry Wilson c1905. The fine stained glass windows of the chancel, including the east window of Christ in Glory, are by Francis Spear, of the early 1950s. The floor of the chancel is dramatic, with bright coloured stone and mosaics, and circular panels in memory of the von Glehn family 1886.

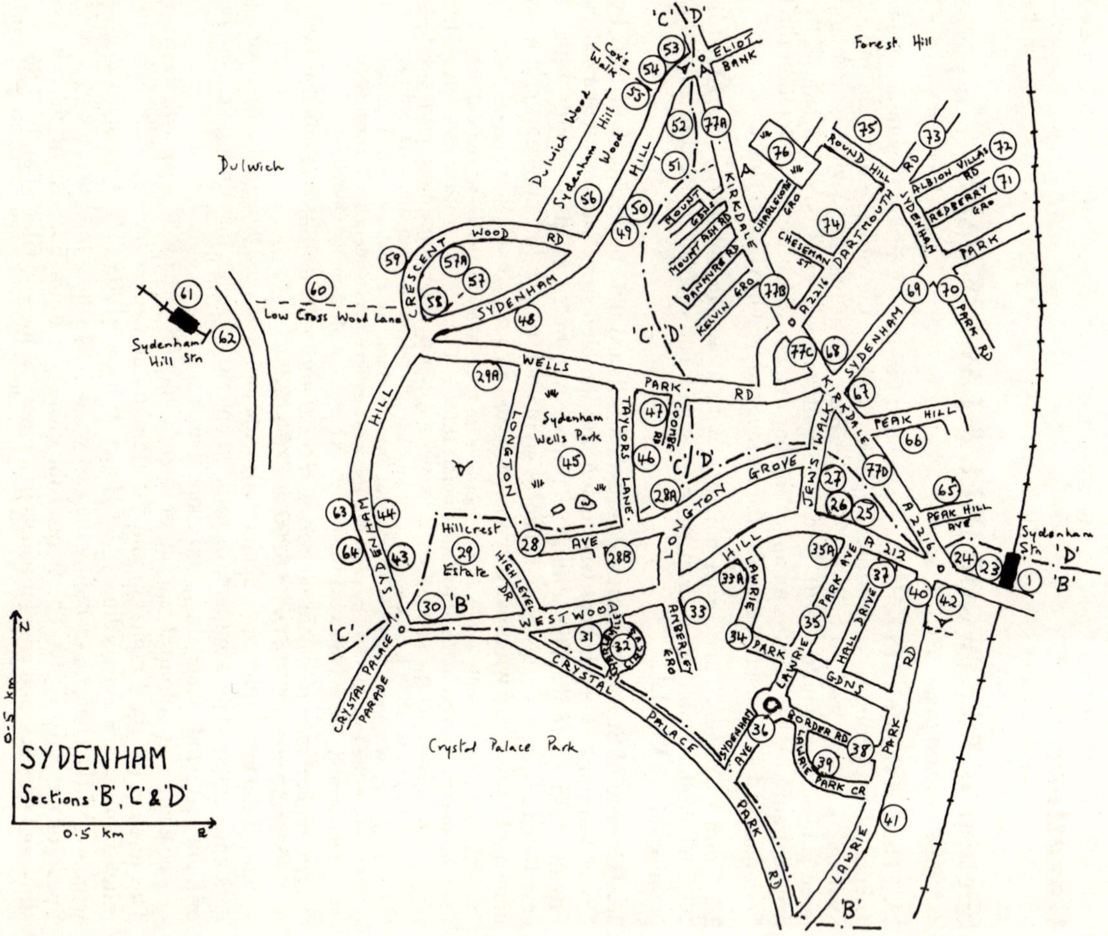

SYDENHAM

Sections 'B', 'C' & 'D'

The stained glass windows along the south aisle are also by Spear. The west window is by Clayton & Bell 1888. Two smaller windows, above the south porch and opposite in the north aisle, are by Burlison & Grylls, probably c1900.

Note also the Gothic pulpit, of 1874, with its intricately carved stonework. The font at the west end is probably c1832, and is notable for the Greek lettering forming a palindrome around the rim.

In the churchyard, in front of the church, note the large tomb to Robert and Elizabeth Harrild 1853 *(see Sydenham 69, 76)*, and a strange tomb in the shape of a miniature church (but not this church) to Charles English 1867, the first vicar of the parish.

26. 12/28 Westwood Hill. No 12, called **St Davids**, next to the church, is a large detached Gothic house of 1872, bearing a blue plaque: 'Sir Ernest Shackleton 1874-1922, Antarctic explorer, lived here'.

The next group, nos 14/28, four pairs with Gothic and Tudor motifs, are older, c1852, and much more distinctive; the pattern continues round the corner in 1/13 Jew's Walk *(see 27)*. Note the gargoyles on nos 18, 20 and 14, and the oriel on no 28. Sir George Grove was the first resident of no 14, before he moved to 208 Sydenham Road *(see Sydenham 8)*.

27. 1/13 Jew's Walk. Jew's Walk is an attractive road, in which two fine groups of houses have survived - nos 1/13 at the southern end (on the east side) in Victorian Tudor / Gothic style, and nos 2/6 at the northern end (on the west side) in Georgian style. *For 2/6 Jew's Walk, see Sydenham 77D.*

> The street was named after a line of elm trees planted in the late 18th century by David Ximenes, who lived in Westwood House, which was located opposite Jew's Walk on the other side of Westwood Hill. Westwood House was built 1766, and used by the Lawrie family in the early 19th century. It was rebuilt by John Pearson 1881 for Henry Littleton (proprietor of the music publisher Novello, the largest business of its kind in the world when he retired in 1887). The house was demolished 1952; the Sheenewood Estate is now on the site. The elms were replaced by chestnuts in the 1850s.

Nos 1/13 is a group of fanciful Gothic / Tudor houses c1852, rather more eccentric than the group round the corner at 14/28 Westwood Hill *(see 26)*. Nos 1/11 are three pairs, some with gargoyles and patterned brick.

> Eleanor Marx, daughter of Karl Marx, lived with Edward Aveling at no 7 from 1895, and committed suicide there in 1898.

No 13, the southernmost house, is large and detached, handsome in bright red brick, with an impressive tower and a recessed Gothic porch.

28. Longton Avenue is an imposing street, which sweeps round the south and west sides of Sydenham Wells Park. Most houses are Edwardian or interwar, not special in themselves, but they have quite an impact overlooking the park.

There are however two interesting groups, at the junctions with Longton Grove **(28A)** and with Ormanton Road **(28B)**:

2/10 Longton Avenue, together with 70/72 Longton Grove, form a fine classical group - nos 2/4 are of 1856; no 6 of 1862; nos 8 and 10 are tall houses, with fine bow windows through three floors, of 1866; 70/72 Longton Grove are c1857.

17 Longton Avenue and the three adjacent houses in Ormanton Road are self-build houses c1982, based on the Walter Segal concept *(see Forest Hill 2)*.

29. Hillcrest Estate. This sprawling estate of 1967, accessed by High Level Drive, occupies a valley below the ridge of Sydenham Hill and between Westwood Hill and Wells Park Road. The blocks and terraces, though uninspired in themselves, are nicely arranged in closes in an evocative rural environment, with steep wooded fragments remaining from the Great North Wood.

At the end of Vigilant Close, at the far point of the estate, is the site of the platforms of **Upper Sydenham Station**, now a flat grassed area leading up to the mouth, with its ornamental brickwork, of the Crescent Wood tunnel, which emerged about 300 metres to the north in Sydenham Hill Wood *(see Sydenham 56)*. A lane leads from here steeply up to the old stationmaster's house cum booking office, of 1884, now **151/159 Wells Park Road (29A)**. The station was opened in 1884 on the Crystal Palace High Level line, which closed 1954 *(see also Crystal Palace 21; Sydenham 56; Forest Hill 7, 19A)*.

At the junction of High Level Drive and Westwood Hill is a Bridge House Estate property marker post of 1816, rather eroded *(see Sydenham 51)*.

30. *Sunnydene, 108 Westwood Hill, a large and strange house designed by John Francis Bentley 1870. The projecting windows on the upper floor are the dominant feature; on the buttress underneath is a sunburst (a motif repeated on a gatepost) and the letters AVE. The gable has herringbone brickwork and an eagle on top, and there is some elaborate brickwork.

The house forms a fine group with the adjacent houses, **nos 106** and **104**, also c1870, but overall more classical in style.

A little further east on Westwood Hill is a tall Bridge House Estate property marker post of 1816 *(see Sydenham 51)*.

31. Caen Tower, 43 Westwood Hill, an extraordinary Gothic house of 1884, with a fanciful tower, gables and oriels. It is on the corner of

32. Charleville Circus. The design of the houses does not measure up to the opportunity presented by this attractive circular layout. There are five pairs on the inner circle, and two groups on the outer circle. All houses are of the 1880s, more or less Gothic in style, except no 13 which is a modern intrusion.

33. Sydenham High School, of the Girls Day School Trust, occupies a large site between Amberley Grove and Lawrie Park Gardens.

> The school opened in 1887 in Longton Hotel, at the junction of Westwood Hill and Longton Grove, and c1934 moved here to Horner Grange, 19 Westwood Hill.

Horner Grange, a fantastic Gothic mansion of 1883, remains the main building of the school. The front has a triple arched entrance flanked by gabled bays; the rear has a similar entrance with a balcony above; both the front and (in winter) the rear are best seen from Amberley Grove. There is a great look-out tower, with wonderful views to the north and east. A ballroom with a minstrel's gallery remains from a mansion of 1874 on the site; it is now the dining-room, and projects to the rear alongside Amberley Grove. Some of the rooms have exotic fireplaces of the 1900s. The main part of the building was badly damaged by fire 1997, and was well restored 1998.

The school also occupies: the former **coach-house and stables** of Horner Grange (now the Technology Centre), in front on Westwood Hill, an extraordinary Gothic building of 1889 designed by Joseph Fogarty, with fanciful gables, turrets and tall chimneys; the former **lodge**, c1887; and **15 Westwood Hill (33A)**, now the Junior

School, a large classical building of 1862. In between these older buildings are a series of interwar and postwar buildings, including a startling red brick block of 1993 along Amberley Grove.

34. Lawrie Park Gardens, on the Lawrie Park Estate, falls into two parts. The part between Westwood Hill and Lawrie Park Avenue was laid out c1863. Remaining from that time are, on the west side, **Ashbourne House**, no 10, a large classical house of 1864, the contrast between its vivid white stone dressings and its lively yellow brick being quite appealing; and on the east side, **no 87**, an attractive stuccoed house, probably of 1864, currently being restored, and **nos 115/123**, of 1866, in poor condition and rather ungainly.

The part between Lawrie Park Avenue and Lawrie Park Road was laid out earlier, c1860. Remaining from that time are two large stuccoed Italianate houses of 1861, **Woolwich House**, no 183, and **no 191**, with a bold porch.

35. *Lawrie Park Avenue, the finest street on the Lawrie Park Estate, highly attractive, wide and spacious with grass verges and many trees; it was laid out in this fashion soon after 1852; it was formerly known as Sydenham Avenue and as The Avenue. The view along the Avenue northwards towards St Bartholomew's Church is impressive; this is the view featured in Camille Pissarro's painting of 1871, 'La Route de Sydenham', which is in the National Gallery *(see also Crystal Palace 20A)*.

At the southern end is a roundabout with the boundary oak, which marked the boundaries of the parishes of St Mary Lewisham and St George Beckenham until 1900, of the boroughs of Lewisham and Beckenham (and of the counties of London and Kent) from 1900 to 1965, and of the boroughs of Lewisham and Bromley since 1965. Beyond the roundabout, the road is still called Sydenham Avenue *(see 36)*.

The only house remaining from the time of Pissarro's painting is **no 53**, facing the roundabout, a large vaguely classical house, probably c1860, but much altered. At the junction of Lawrie Park Avenue and Westwood Hill, Pissarro shows Dunedin House, of 1859; the present building on the site, **Burnage Court (35A)**, 7 Westwood Hill, is a rebuild of 1888, large, irregular and rambling, gloomy in its dark red brick, with a tower, gables and tiled frontages. The design of the more modern houses (and of the older houses too) conspicuously fails to measure up to the grandeur of the street.

36. Sydenham Avenue is the continuation of Lawrie Park Avenue *(see 35)* to the south in the London Borough of Bromley, and maintains its grandeur. Some older buildings have survived.

Summerfield, no 6, on the east side, looks like a long low stuccoed Regency house, but was originally a pair of outbuildings for two houses of the 1850s; the outbuildings were joined together, probably in the late 19th century.

Opposite on the west side note **nos 3/9**, a group of four large and stately detached houses, remaining from a larger group c1885, similar in style but alternately red brick and stock brick.

Further along, on the east side, is **Brooklyn Cottage**, almost hidden behind a barrier of trees and shrubs; it was originally the coach-house and stables for Southwood Lodge (later called Brooklyn), built 1859, demolished 1998.

37. Hall Drive was originally largely a carriage drive leading to Sydenham Hall, an old house rebuilt c1805 for the Lawrie family, replaced by nos 15/19 in 1939. It is an attractive road, with grass verges, white railings and posts. **No 36**, near the southern end, looks like a small Regency stuccoed house, but was originally the lodge for a house c1862; it then became a separate house, with extensions which have now gone, in the late 19th century.

38. Border Road retains on the north side two mid 19th century pairs, nos 2/2a and 16/18, substantially altered and not very appealing.

39. *Lawrie Park Crescent preserves more of its original houses than any other street on the Lawrie Park Estate. It originally comprised four large stuccoed pairs of the late 1850s and one smaller house in the middle. Three of the four pairs have survived - 82/84 Lawrie Park Road, much altered 1900; nos 2/4 and no 10, relatively unaltered and quite handsome; the last pair, on the west corner with Border Road, as well as the smaller house have gone.

40. Lawrie Park Road, marking the eastern boundary of the Lawrie Park Estate. From north to south, note:

At the junction with Westwood Hill, **no 2** is a large and rambling stuccoed Italianate villa c1861 but much altered, with a central tower over a Tuscan porch. The ground floor is rusticated, with square-headed windows; the windows on the upper floors are round-headed. *(For Old Cedars opposite, see 42.)*

A short way down, on the east side, between Cricketers Walk and Bays Close, is a modern block with a Lewisham Council plaque: 'W. G. Grace 1848-1915 cricketer lived in a house on this site'. Grace lived here from 1899 before moving to Mottingham in 1909.

Between Bays Close and Copeman Close is a sequence of large stately houses of the late 1880s with strong gables. Next is St Christopher's Hospice *(see 41)*.

On the west side, just beyond Lawrie Park Gardens, **nos 74/76** are a large Italianate stuccoed pair of 1857, but altered and with later extensions.

(For nos 82/84, see 39, under Lawrie Park Crescent.)

Towards the southern end, on the east side, is **Lichfield House**, no 79, an attractive stuccoed villa of the late 1850s with a Corinthian porch.

41. St Christopher's Hospice, 51/59 Lawrie Park Road, a large complex.

> It was a pioneering venture when founded by Dame Cicely Saunders in 1967, and is now regarded as the world leader of the modern hospice movement.

The main block is of 1967, weatherboarded and glazed, attractive with staggered bays and a curving top storey. To the south is Albertine Centre, consisting of a house of the late 1920s connected to the main building by a linking block of 1991. Further south is a separate modern building of 1972, the Education Centre.

42. Old Cedars, Westwood Hill, a large house which is in part late 18th century, now a nursing home. The front view shows, from left to right: the dominant section, of the 1860s, including a canted bay and the attractive entrance porch; the original house of the early 1770s consisting of four bays plus the ground floor only of the next bay; and a large neo-Georgian extension of 1992 which also covers the one storey part of the original house. To the left of the house are the Georgian coach-house and stables. The rear, visible from Raymond Close, shows clearly the original house of the early 1770s with elegant twin full-height bows, flanked to the left by the postwar extension and to the right by a canted bay of the 1860s.

SYDENHAM

Gazetteer

Section 'C' SYDENHAM HILL & WELLS PARK
(See map on page 18)

*Sydenham Hill. This amazing road, over a kilometre in length, sweeps round in an inverted S curve along a ridge, over 100 metres high, which forms the Lewisham / Southwark boundary. The land falls away steeply on both sides. It is an ancient highway; Roman objects were found in a gravel pit here in 1806. The land to the west is part of the Dulwich Estate. There were a few houses here in the early 19th century, by the 1860s there were many; a few have survived, others are replaced by large housing estates or blocks of flats.

The sequence of locations starts at the mini roundabout at the junction of Sydenham Hill and Westwood Hill, then follows the east side of Sydenham Hill, with a diversion along Wells Park Road; it returns along the west side, with a diversion to Sydenham Hill Station and St Stephens Church. The even numbers of Sydenham Hill are on the east side, the odd numbers on the west side.

43. Grange Court, 12 Sydenham Hill, a substantial and imposing classical house c1861, with great round-headed windows on three levels and nice decorative details.

44. *16 Sydenham Hill, formerly known as **The Wood**, a long and intriguing mansion in Tudor style. The central gabled part is linked on either side by low irregular sections to similar gabled end pavilions. As a whole, it looks almost symmetrical, but the building history is complicated.

The original building is of c1840, but substantial extensions to the left of c1855 (designed by Sir Joseph Paxton for Lady Hunloke, mistress of his patron the Duke of Devonshire) and to the right of c1896 have produced the present house, almost like a palace. The frontage consists of, from left to right: a gabled pavilion c1855; a lower section and the central gabled bay of the original house c1840; a lower section and a gabled pavilion c1896. The old coach-house to the left at the rear is basically c1840, but altered later.

The neighbouring houses are also of interest, and together they form a fine varied group. To the north, **18 Sydenham Hill**, a stuccoed Regency villa with a good porch, probably c1840. To the south, **14 Sydenham Hill**, a handsome house with a Gothic porch between bargeboarded gabled bays, probably c1860, now being restored.

45. *Sydenham Wells Park. This attractive park, opened 1901, has in the north spacious rolling parkland, and in the south, two ponds, fed by springs, which are now the only visible manifestation of Sydenham Wells *(see Introduction, pages 9-10)*.

46. 69/71 Taylors Lane, a pair of old cottages, with weatherboarded upper storey, probably basically of the 1820s. Much altered since, well restored recently.

47. St Philip the Apostle Church, Coombe Road. This low-lying church of 1983, with its steeply raked back roof, occupies the eastern half of the site of the original St Philips Church (built by Edwin Nash 1865, demolished 1982); the rest of the site now forms part of the Wells Park Estate. An enclosed garden outside has a bell and a crucifix from the old church. The interior *(contact 122 Wells Park Road or 0181-699 4930)* has a fine modern altar, font and lectern, and from the old church, a statue of Christ the King and ceramic Stations of the Cross (interwar, attributed to the workshop of Eric Gill).

Wells Park Hall, a Gothic building to the north, was built by Edwin Nash c1870 as St Philips School; it is now Sydenham Seventh Day Adventist Church.

Nearby on Wells Park Road are two pleasant pubs, **Duke of Edinburgh**, no 104, of 1866, and **The Talma**, no 109, of 1863.

48. Highfield, 28 Sydenham Hill, a small classical house c1855.

49. The Cedars, 34 Sydenham Hill, an enormous classical mansion built for Charles Ash Body 1898. To the left of the entrance porch the internal staircase windows are encased in amazing stonework, forming an ornamental tableau which incorporates the monogram CAB. The end bay on the right has a finely decorated pediment.

50. Sydenham Hill House, 34a Sydenham Hill, an irregular mock-Jacobean house of 1898. Above the entrance is a tower with a battlemented double storey oriel and an odd parapet, and on either side are gabled wings, one with a double storey oriel.

51. *Lammas Green, a highly attractive estate with a village atmosphere, designed for the City of London Corporation by Donald McMorran 1957. A circular green, with a cedar tree, is surrounded on three sides by low white terraces, and on the other side by a taller brick block. The blocks facing Sydenham Hill have less appeal. Note the Corporation of London lamppost 1878 at the entrance to the green, and further along a **Bridge House Estate** property marker 1816. On the other side of the green, on the footpath leading to Kirkdale, is another Bridge House Estate marker 1816.

> The income from the Bridge House Estate paid for and maintains the four bridges owned by the Corporation of London - London Bridge, Blackfriars Bridge, Southwark Bridge, Tower Bridge. The estate originated with a bequest for the upkeep of the old London Bridge completed in 1201, the other bridges of course being centuries later.

52. Castlebar, 46 Sydenham Hill, a long mansion of 1879, now a nursing home. The scale is enormous, but the design and detailing are uninspired. The Ionic porch is too shallow, and the tower above unimaginative, though there is a separate tower leading up to a tall and narrow roof which is the sole exciting feature.

53. 133 & 135 Sydenham Hill are a very interesting and attractive pair. The central recessed part of no 133 is part of Holly Brow, an early 19th century house; the bowed section to the right and the section to the left were added in the mid 19th century. Behind, no 135, still called **Holly Brow**, is the other part of the early 19th century house, extended and stuccoed. Holly Brow was made into two houses probably between the wars. From the roundabout at this point there is a fine view over London.

54. Pantiles, 131 Sydenham Hill, looks like an early 19th century Georgian house, but is in fact modern, c1932. It is elegant and harmonious. There is a St Giles Camberwell parish marker of 1870 just inside the gateway.

55. *Cox's Walk is a pleasant rural lane lined by oaks, cut through the woods in the early 18th century. The walk goes from Sydenham Hill alongside Sydenham Hill Wood, steadily and then steeply down to ***Cox's Walk footbridge**, then continues down to the junction of Lordship Lane and Dulwich Common.

The present footbridge is of 1908, though there was a bridge over the railway from 1865. Thick woodland and shrubbery now obscure the view from the bridge in Camille Pissarro's painting of 1871 of Lordship Lane Station, in the Courtauld Institute Galleries *(see Crystal Palace 20A)*; the station closed in 1954.

56. *Sydenham Hill Wood. This, together with Dulwich Wood to the west, forms the largest surviving fragment of the Great North Wood. It is now a unique mix of woodland and bits of Victorian gardens. It has been managed by the London Wildlife Trust since 1982. Highly attractive, with firm winding paths on a steep hillside; some steep ascents and descents are involved.

It is accessible via Cox's Walk footbridge *(see 55)*, but is best entered from Crescent Wood Road. A path to the left leads quickly but steeply down to and alongside the parapet over the red brick tunnel entrance of Crescent Wood Tunnel, which emerges about 300 metres to the south at the site of Upper Sydenham Station *(see Sydenham 29)* on the Crystal Palace High Level Railway, opened 1865, closed 1954. *(See also Crystal Palace 21; Sydenham 29; Forest Hill 7, 19A.)* The old track-bed is now followed by a narrow footpath, which continues till at the end it goes up and onto the footbridge; from the bridge, Cox's Walk leads uphill to Sydenham Hill.

The footbridge can also be reached by taking the first path to the right, passing first a great Cedar of Lebanon in a large clearing, then to the left a garden folly consisting of a broken fragment of stone archway, and continuing to the footbridge.

A row of green posts parallel with the track-bed separates Sydenham Hill Wood from Dulwich Wood, which is managed by the Dulwich Estate.

57. *Beltwood, 41 Sydenham Hill, is a large, spectacular and somewhat eccentric mansion c1854, set in large grounds which occupy much of the space between Sydenham Hill and Crescent Wood Road. However, the house is at the end of a driveway, and is difficult to see from the road over the hedges.

The porch, at the side of the house, has four Ionic columns and bow windows above on either side. Note that the volutes of the Ionic columns are square rather than curved, a motif which re-occurs on the Ionic pilasters of the lodge, also c1854, by the road. The house has a magnificent facade facing south - the projecting central section has two small bow windows and is topped by a large pediment (with a circular window and Wedgwood style classical decoration), and on either side are large fully glazed bow windows.

At the rear, **Crescent Wood Cottage (57A)**, stuccoed with a turret, set back down a lane from Crescent Wood Road, was an outbuilding of Beltwood, probably also c1854.

58. *Dulwich Wood House, 39 Sydenham Hill, a handsome stuccoed pub, Italianate, built 1858. It has a central square lookout tower with polygonal bayed ranges splayed out on either side.

59. Crescent Wood Road. This road sweeps round to enclose an oval-shaped plateau on the ridge of Sydenham Hill. At the eastern end is Sydenham Hill Wood (see 56). At the western end are Low Cross Wood Lane (see 60) and some interesting houses. At the junction with Sydenham Hill, note the St Giles Camberwell iron parish marker of 1870.

On the north side: **No 1**, formerly called Lyncombe, a massive Gothic red brick house with Dutch gables, of the late 1860s, with a lodge in front in similar style.

No 3 is in Georgian style, also of the late 1860s. It has a blue plaque: 'John Logie Baird 1888-1946 television pioneer lived here'. Baird lived here 1934-46, and invented the colour television receiver in his laboratory here.

On the south side: ***Six Pillars**, a Corbusian house of 1935 by Val Harding, of the Tecton team founded by Berthold Lubetkin in the 1930s. Six yellow pillars support a blank white upper floor with a narrow horizontal band of windows, and a white roof parapet with a balcony opening onto a central round brick staircase tower.

Nos 2 and **4** are similar large Gothic red brick houses, of the late 1860s.

60. Low Cross Wood Lane, a delightful footpath, wide but very steep, leads down from Crescent Wood Road to Sydenham Hill Station and St Stephens Church.

61. *Sydenham Hill Station, opened 1863, in a wonderfully picturesque and rural location in a cutting with wooded slopes on all sides. From College Road a covered walkway leads quite steeply down to a lattice bridge, probably c1900, from which covered walkways lead to the two platforms. To the east is the red brick tunnel entrance to the Penge Tunnel, two kilometres long (see also Sydenham 3).

62. *Church of St Stephen, College Road, the parish church of South Dulwich. A Gothic ragstone church built 1868-75 by Banks & Barry. The church has a powerful impact - a very tall broach spire on top of a bold tower seems to dwarf the nave and apsed chancel, and the steep roof, with its clerestory of gabled dormer windows, bears down on the low aisle windows. Note the unusual tracery in all the windows, and the ornate frieze below the west window.

The church is normally open Mondays, Wednesdays, Fridays; otherwise contact the vicarage opposite or phone 0181-766 7281.

The ***interior** is tall and splendid. It is also very colourful because of the chancel roof looking bright and blue ahead, the stencilling in the roof, the painted angels above the chancel arch, and the white patterns on the dark roof timbers. In the chancel the east window is by C. E. Kempe (the only prewar stained glass remaining), and there is a mural of the trial and stoning of St Stephen by Sir Edward Poynter 1872. The west window has stained glass of St Stephen and St Paul by Moira Forsyth 1952, and under it a small nativity triptych by Charles Gurrey.

63. 17 Sydenham Hill, formerly called Dilkhoosh, is a substantial classical house, probably c1860, with a classical colonnade added in the later 19th century.

64. 11 Sydenham Hill, with its fine porch and fanlight, looks like an early 19th century Regency villa, but is actually late 19th century.

SYDENHAM

Gazetteer

Section 'D' KIRKDALE & SYDENHAM PARK
(See map on page 18)

65. Peak Hill Avenue has on both sides large Italianate pairs of the late 1860s.

66. Peak Hill has on the south side a long and handsome terrace of Edwardian houses of 1905 in a staggered pattern following the curve in the road. The houses have crow-stepped gables with scrolls and interesting terracotta carvings around the doorways.

67. Church of the Resurrection, a Roman Catholic church of 1974 in pale brick, with just a few narrow windows. The statue of the Risen Christ over the entrance is by Steven Sykes.

The **interior** *(contact the adjoining Presbytery, or phone 0181-291 5766)* is mainly top-lit and contains an impressive crucifix by Elspeth Reid.

68. Park Hall, Sydenham Park, was built in 1850 in an extravagantly Gothic style as a congregational chapel, but since 1867 has been used as a sunday school and by other organisations; it is now a fitness centre.

69. *Sydenham Park was developed from 1842 as part of the Sydenham Park Estate on the site of a reservoir for the Croydon Canal. A number of fine classical houses of the 1840s and 1850s have survived on both sides, and the western part of the street is highly attractive.

The north side begins from the west with a series of notable houses of the 1840s: **nos 3/5**, **7/9** and **11/13**, similar stuccoed pairs c1843, some with later bays; **nos 15/17**, a stuccoed pair; **nos 19/21**, a brick pair; **nos 23** and **25**, fine detached stuccoed houses with bold Doric porches; **nos 27/29**, a brick pair. Further along, **nos 37/43**, originally two pairs c1847 made into a terrace c1860 with a series of pilaster strips.

Near the junction with Sydenham Park Road, Trinity Court is a pleasing block of flats c1985, on the site of Holy Trinity Church (built 1866, demolished c1984). In front, a statue remains from the old church; and, on an old wall, are some fragments of property stones (on which can be seen the names of Robert Harrild, a major developer of the Sydenham Park Estate, and Mary Baxter - *see 76*). To the west, Trinity Path leads to Trinity Church Hall, a low red brick building of 1924, now serving as the church.

The south side is perhaps even more impressive; it begins from the west with a series of houses of the 1840s and 1850s which form a harmonious group. **Nos 2/6**, a highly attractive group of 1856 with a fine porch in the central house and recessed porches on either side; **nos 8/10** and **nos 12/14**, two imposing pairs of the 1840s; **nos 16/18**, of the early 1850s, linked to **nos 20/22** c1855, two pairs with stuccoed and rusticated ground floors; **nos 26/28** and **nos 30/32**, two tall pairs with fine Ionic porches c1843, the latter pair stuccoed.

Beyond the junction with Sydenham Park Road, note **nos 68/70**, a large stuccoed Italianate pair c1845.

At the end a footbridge over the railway leads to Dacres Road, Forest Hill, and to the Dietrich Bonhoeffer Church *(see Forest Hill 49)*.

70. Sydenham Park Road, like Sydenham Park, was developed as part of the Sydenham Park Estate on the site of a reservoir for the Croydon Canal.

On the west side of the street, an outstanding group of five large villas of the 1840s and 1850s have survived. **No 14** has a Tudor porch with castellated turrets, a steep Gothic gable above, and Tudor windows. The other four are classical: **Helix House**, no 16, is Italianate with a porch; **no 18** has an attractive Ionic porch; **no 20**, of 1855, has a fine doorcase with a Gibbs surround, and a Lewisham Council plaque 'Richard Jefferies 1848-1887 nature writer and novelist lived here'; **no 22** is smaller with a fine Doric porch.

At the junction with Sydenham Park is **Park Mansions**, which consists of a mid 19th century Italianate pair, identifiable by the corner quoins facing Sydenham Park Road, extended and much enlarged on both sides in 1906. Beyond the junction, **no 59** is of 1843, with a porch featuring female heads added later.

71. Redberry Grove is a private road off Sydenham Park Road with white gates and posts; it can become quite muddy.

Nos 2/3, called Redberry House and Elmfield respectively, are a splendid stuccoed pair with great gables and a Gothic doorway, of the late 1840s.

Arden, no 4, is a detached villa with a fine Doric doorcase, of the late 1840s.

72. *Albion Villas Road, a lane off Sydenham Park Road.

Nos 3/4 and **5/6** are two great handsome stuccoed pairs c1847, with rusticated ground floors; nos 5/6 was Sydenham Childrens Hospital from 1872 to 1885.

Nos 7/8, c1850, has a stuccoed and rusticated ground floor.

At the end, **nos 9** and **10** are two houses c1885 with tiled upper floors, in a rural Arts & Crafts style.

Opposite, a millennium green is being created on the site of an old tennis club.

73. Dartmouth Road is partly in Sydenham and partly in Forest Hill *(see also Forest Hill 20-23)*. The southern part, together with the adjoining part of Kirkdale *(see 77C)*, is the original 19th century shopping centre of Sydenham.

On the east side, going from north to south, between Sydenham Park Road and Kirkdale:

Nos 165/175, a fine Italianate terrace c1843, made up of pairs linked by adjoining recessed porches; this was part of the Sydenham Park Estate *(see 69)*.

Bricklayers Arms, no 189, a pub of 1924, well restored in 1998, with a fine large plaque on the side: 'Youngs, The Ram Brewery, Wandsworth, established 1831'.

On the west side, going from south to north, between Kirkdale and Thorpewood Avenue, which marks the beginning of Forest Hill:
In **Cheseman Street**, note **no 7**, a small detached house of the 1830s.
For Sydenham School, see 74.
Courtside, set back behind a modern terrace, was originally two large and handsome houses of 1857; in 1923 they were linked together and modern extensions built on either side, making one long group. It is best seen from Round Hill.
Round Hill Lodge, no 104, on the corner of Round Hill, a pleasing house of the 1820s, which was the lodge for Round Hill House *(see 75)*.
Nos 88/90, an impressive Italianate pair c1842.
Holy Trinity School, a Gothic building of 1874.

74. Sydenham School, a large complex with three main buildings directly facing Dartmouth Road. From left to right, first is a large modernist concrete block by Sir Basil Spence of 1957; it is supported by tapering piers on the ground floor, which was originally open but was enclosed in 1994. Then a low modern block of 1973 containing the library and sixth form centre; to its left, in the gap between the buildings, the school hall by Spence can be seen far back. Then the original building, large and stately, classical, red brick, with a rounded porch, of 1917, extended 1921.

> Sydenham School was founded in Westbourne Drive, Forest Hill, in the 1860s. It moved to 4/6 Manor Mount *(see Forest Hill 17)* in 1875. The building was acquired by the London County Council in 1905 and renamed Sydenham County Secondary School. It moved to this site in 1917.

75. *St Antholin's spire, off Round Hill. This octagonal spire, now sited between two modern terraces, was the upper part of the steeple of the Church of St Antholin, Watling Street, one of Sir Christopher Wren's city churches, built in the Gothic style between 1678 and 1688. It was moved to the grounds of Round Hill House (a house of the 1820s, demolished in the 1860s) by the owner Robert Harrild *(see 76)* as a folly c1850, when the church spire was replaced; the church itself was demolished in 1875. Note the Sydenham Society plaque of 1987.

76. Baxter Field. This open space, in a sort of valley, was named after George Baxter, a pioneer of colour printing. Note the Sydenham Society plaque of 1980 on the west side of the field.

> George Baxter (1804-1867) developed a method of printing in oil colours, patented in 1835, which was more successful than previous methods. He married Mary Harrild, daughter of Robert Harrild, in 1827. He was killed in an accident in 1867 and is buried at Christ Church, Forest Hill *(see Forest Hill 41)*.'
> Robert Harrild (1780-1853), of Round Hill House, was an innovative manufacturer of printing equipment. He was a major developer of the Sydenham Park Estate. He died in 1853, and is buried in St Bartholomews Church *(see Sydenham 25)*.

77. *Kirkdale cuts through the middle of the old Sydenham Common. It descends steeply from the roundabout at the junction of Sydenham Hill and Eliot Bank, providing fantastic views to the south. The roads on the west side north of Halifax Street are all culs-de-sac. Around the junction with Dartmouth Road is a minor shopping centre, which in the 19th century was the main shopping centre of Sydenham. From here Kirkdale continues until it reaches Westwood Hill, near Sydenham Station.

> Because of the abundance of buildings of interest, the entries for Kirkdale and some roads leading off it are split into four blocks, going from north to south. In Kirkdale, the even street numbers are on the west side, and the odd street numbers are on the east side. All the locations listed in the third and fourth blocks are on the west side of Kirkdale.

From Eliot Bank to Mount Gardens (77A):
 Eliot Bank is not made up and can become muddy at times. At the junction with Kirkdale is a Lewisham Parish boundary stone of 1859. To the left **Oak Cottage** has dramatic twin gables and Tudor windows; the left half is of the early 1850s, and was the lodge for houses in Eliot Bank, the right half was added in similar style in the late 19th century. Opposite is a terrace of 1982, **Julian Taylor Path**, which curls round the corner and copies the motifs of Oak Cottage. Beyond on the right is **Phoenix House**, a large and impressive house with Tudor windows and a tower over a Gothic doorway, of 1855.
 ***Eliot Lodge**, on the east side. The gatepost to the left, with its irregular pattern of stone and coloured brick, is a forewarning of the dominant feature of the house, the extraordinary and exotic slim octagonal tower with its tapering top. The entrance block and the two flanking gabled bays and tower are c1853, the much taller block beyond is an extension c1870. The house is very large, very Gothic, with a multitude of gables and odd corners.
 A footpath on the west side, with a Bridge House Estate property marker of 1816, leads to Lammas Green, a Corporation of London estate *(see Sydenham 51)*.
 No 24, c1820, with a fine Ionic porch.
 ***Mount Gardens** starts as one narrow lane, then splits in two, with another lane leading off to the right; it preserves throughout an extraordinary rural quality, unique in the area. Taking the lane straight ahead, note: **The Cottage / Lynton Cottage**, a pair of the 1820s; **Oak House**, a large and remarkable Edwardian house c1900, with an upper floor supported on Ionic pillars; and, in large grounds, **The Orchard**, basically of the 1830s but altered and extended. Taking the lane to the right, note: ***Ashtree Cottage / Rouselle Cottage**, a weather-boarded pair c1816; **Hazeldine Cottage**, originally the staff quarters for a large house in Sydenham Hill of the 1860s, made into a separate house in the late 19th century, with steeply gabled porch and dormers, and a late Victorian wall letter box inset into the porch; and at the end, **The Chalet**, of the 1830s, which cannot be seen properly.

From Mount Gardens to Dartmouth Road (77B):
 Mount Ash Road has on both sides similar long terraces c1870.
 Nos 46/48, a large pair, with fine porches on either side, probably of the late 1840s.
 20/22 Panmure Road, a large pair of the late 1840s.

Charlecote Grove preserves a number of houses basically of 1838: **no 2**, with late 19th century additions including a porch with an oriel and the extension to the south; **Percy Cottage**; and **nos 14/16**.

The former **Sydenham Public Lecture Hall**, Kelvin Grove, facing Kirkdale, a large building with an arcaded Italian Renaissance front with polychrome decoration. It was built in 1861 by Henry Dawson based on a design by Sir Joseph Paxton; it was used as a lecture hall and also as a school for the British and Foreign Bible Schools Society, and is now New Woodlands School. The extensions on either side with great chimneys and bay windows are c1900.

Behind is **Kelvin Grove School**, a large multi-gabled London School Board building of 1876, originally Sydenham Hill School; the separate smaller building to the north was added by the London County Council after 1902.

9/15 Kelvin Grove, an impressive Italianate group, one pair and five detached houses, of 1863.

*****Nos 89/91**, a fine pair of weather-boarded cottages of the 1820s.

From Dartmouth Road to Jew's Walk (77C):

The Woodman, no 110, originally a building c1831, which became a pub in the 1840s and was rebuilt in the 1850s.

*****Halifax Street.** This street preserves an authentic atmosphere as it bends round to join Wells Park Road. There are pairs of cottages c1849, and terraces of double-fronted houses and an Italianate terrace of the early 1850s.

Nos 122/130, a stuccoed early 19th century group, all except no 128 marred by modern projecting shopfronts; no 126 has a canted oriel.

High Street Buildings, nos 134/142, a shopping development c1895, a fanciful red brick block with lots of pinnacles and terracotta work.

Fox & Hounds, no 150, a pub originally of 1824 but rebuilt 1894.

*****Farnboro House**, no 152, a superb stuccoed villa c1840; the Doric porch has fluted columns, and there is a very bold ground floor bow to the left.

From Jew's Walk to Westwood Hill (77D):

2/6 Jew's Walk, a fine group of three classical villas. *****Grove Centre House**, no 2, probably of the late 1840s, very handsome, has an Ionic porch with fluted columns; it now serves as offices for The Grove Centre next door (Sydenham United Free Church, a low flat building of 1974, replacing the Congregational Church-in-the-Grove of 1867, demolished 1972). **Whitehead House**, no 4, of the early 1850s, has a Corinthian porch and end brick pilasters with Corinthian stone capitals. **No 6**, probably of the early 1850s, has fluted Doric columns inside square projecting bays. *For 1/13 Jew's Walk, see Sydenham 27.*

On the corner of Jew's Walk and Kirkdale, a **monument** in baroque style of 1897, commemorating the diamond jubilee of Queen Victoria, designed by Alexander Hennell, restored 1977.

Nos 168/178, Italianate pairs of the early 1850s. (No 174 was briefly the home of the conductor August Manns, *see Crystal Palace Introduction, page 36.*)

No 180/182 is in Gothic style with Tudor doorcases, of the early 1850s.

For Cobb's Corner and The Greyhound, see Sydenham 23-24.

SYDENHAM

Suggested Walks

It is recommended that the suggested walks be followed in conjunction with the Gazetteer and the maps, and that the Gazetteer be consulted at each location for a detailed description. Most locations described in the Gazetteer are covered; some other locations have not been included, as they might add too much to the length of the walks.

Walk no 1 covers Section 'A', Walk no 2 Section 'B', Walk no 3 Section 'C', and Walk no 4 Section 'D'. The walks follow a more or less circular route, so can be joined at any location. All walks begin and end at Sydenham Station except Walk no 3, which can be considered an extension to Walk No 2, beginning and ending at the mini roundabout at the junction of Westwood Hill and Sydenham Hill.

WALK no 1 (including Sydenham Road, Bell Green and the Pool River Walk). Distance approx 3 kilometres.

Try to make an advance arrangement - see the gazetteer- to view the interior of All Saints Church.

On leaving **Sydenham Station (1)**, walk down Station Approach to Silverdale, turn right to Sydenham Road, cross the road, then continue along the south side. After passing Newlands Park, note **32/34 Sydenham Road (4)**. Continue, passing **Golden Lion (5)**, to Trewsbury Road, turn right for the entrance to **All Saints Church (6)** - it is important to see the interior if at all possible. Return to Sydenham Road, noting **All Saints Hall** on the corner.

Continue along the south side of Sydenham Road, passing **nos 120/122 (6)**, **The Prince Alfred** and **Watlington Grove (7)**, until you reach the **Church of Our Lady & St Philip Neri (8)**; note the presbytery and try to see the interior of the Church. After a short distance you come to **Sydenham Library (9)**, then continue to the great traffic junction. Cross the road, noting **Haseltine School (11)** to the right, to **The Old Bath House** and **The Bell (10)**.

Cross the road towards **Savacentre (14)** then continue along Southend Lane until you are opposite **Railway Tavern (12A)**. At this point you can join the **Pool River Walk (13)**. Follow the walk to the end crossing the large bridge, then return to the bridge, walk behind Savacentre, with the two gas holders of **Sydenham Gas Works (15)** on the right, until you reach the street called Bell Green. Turn right for **Livesey Memorial Hall** and **War Memorial (16)**, noting the **Church of the God of Prophecy (17)** opposite. Cross the road, bear round back to Sydenham Road and proceed along the north side.

On reaching Champion Road, turn right for **St Michaels School** and **Church (18)**, then return to Sydenham Road. Continue, passing **no 215 (19)**, to Mayow Road, where the shops originally known as **Grand Parade (22)** start. Continue, making a

32/34 Sydenham Road (early 18th century) - *Sydenham 4*

All Saints Hall (probably c1760) - *Sydenham 6*

The Greyhound (c1870) - *Sydenham 23*

**Church of St Bartholomew
(Lewis Vulliamy 1832, Edwin Nash 1858)** - *Sydenham 25*

16 Sydenham Hill (c1840, Sir Joseph Paxton c1855, c1896)
- *Sydenham 44*

Lammas Green (Donald McMorran 1957) - *Sydenham 51*

Cox's Walk footbridge (1908) - *Sydenham 55*

Beltwood (c1854) - *Sydenham 57*

Dulwich Wood House (1858) - *Sydenham 58*

Six Pillars (Val Harding 1935) - *Sydenham 59*

**St Antholin's Spire
(Sir Christopher Wren 1678-1688)**
- *Sydenham 75*

89/91 Kirkdale (1820s) - *Sydenham 77A*

Farnboro House (c1840) - *Sydenham 77C*

Grove Centre House (late 1840s) - *Sydenham 77D*

Paxton's bust (William Frederick Woodington 1859)
- *Crystal Palace 8*

Lower Terrace (1854) & television transmitter (1954)
- *Crystal Palace 4, 7*

The Iguanodons (Waterhouse Hawkins 1854) - *Crystal Palace 16*

Horniman Conservatory (1894) - *Forest Hill 19*

St Augustines Church (William Oakley 1873, 1887, 1894)
- *Forest Hill 4*

Ashberry Cottage (1820s) - *Forest Hill 14*

**Christ Church
(Ewan Christian 1854, 1885)**
- Forest Hill 40

**67/77 London Road
(late 1840s, c1900)**
- Forest Hill 26

Dietrich Bonhoeffer Church (G S Agar 1959) - *Forest Hill 49*

Dacres Road Nature Reserve - *Forest Hill 48*

Catford Centre (Owen Luder 1969-73) - *Catford 13*

Black Horse & Harrow (1897) - *Catford 15*

Lewisham Theatre (Bradshaw Gass & Hope 1932)
- *Catford 23*

60/62 Ravensbourne Park (cl830) - *Catford 26B*

Homebase Store (Harold Hamilton 1984) - *Catford 44*

St Swithuns Vicarage (Ernest Newton c1892)
- *Hither Green 9*

St Fillans Road (1898) - *Hither Green 19*

Grove Park Hospital (Thomas Dinwiddy 1902) - *Grove Park 5*

detour up Queensthorpe Road for a look at the **Thorpe Estate (21)**, until you are back at Sydenham Station.

WALK no 2 (including Westwood Hill, Hillcrest Estate and the Lawrie Park Estate). Distance approx 4 kilometres.

Try to make an advance arrangement - see the gazetteer- to view the interior of St Bartholomews Church.

On leaving **Sydenham Station (1)**, walk down Station Approach to Silverdale, turn right to Sydenham Road, then right again. Pass **The Fewterer & Firkin (23)**, formerly The Greyhound, and **Cobb's Corner (24)** before proceeding along the north side of Westwood Hill. You soon come to the **Church of St Bartholomew (25)** - it is important to see the interior if at all possible. You then come to **12/28 Westwood Hill (26)**, and round the corner **1/13 Jews Walk (27)**; return to Westwood Hill.

Continue for some considerable distance up Westwood Hill until you come to High Level Close. Turn right into **Hillcrest Estate (29)** and at the end of Vigilant Close, you reach the site of **Upper Sydenham Station**. Return to Westwood Hill, and continue to **nos 104/106** and **Sunnydene (30)**, which is by the junction with Sydenham Hill.

At this point you can, if you have time and energy, take Walk no 3 along Sydenham Hill. If not, retrace steps down Westwood Hill, and after passing the junction with Crystal Palace Park Road, cross to the south side of Westwood Hill. Note **Caen Tower (31)** on the corner of **Charleville Circus (32)**, then walk right round the Circus and continue down Westwood Hill. Detour along Amberley Grove to see the main building of **Sydenham High School (33)** on the left. On reaching **Lawrie Park Gardens (34)**, turn right - you are now on the Lawrie Park Estate.

At the junction with **Lawrie Park Avenue (35)**, turn left - you now have the view, with St Bartholomews Church at the end, in Pissarro's celebrated painting. Walk to the end of the street, noting **Burnage Court (35A)** at the junction with Westwood Hill; retrace steps, passing Lawrie Park Gardens, to the roundabout and the boundary oak. Continue along **Sydenham Avenue (36)** as far as **Brooklyn Cottage**. Return to the roundabout, turn right into **Border Road (38),** and right again into **Lawrie Park Crescent (39)**, which leads to **Lawrie Park Road (40)**.

Opposite is **St Christopher's Hospice (41)**. Turn left up Lawrie Park Road, passing **nos 82/84 (39)** and **nos 72/74**. Detour along **Lawrie Park Gardens (34)** for **no 191** and **Woolwich House**, and for **36 Hall Drive (37)**. At the beginning of Raymond Close on the right, you can see over the fence the twin bows of the rear of **Old Cedars (42)**. At the junction with Westwood Hill, note **2 Lawrie Park Road (40A)**. Turn right, passing the front of **Old Cedars**, and you reach Sydenham Station.

WALK no 3 (including Sydenham Hill, Sydenham Wells Park, Crescent Wood Road and Sydenham Hill Wood). This walk can be considered an extension to Walk no 2, beginning and ending at the mini roundabout at the junction of Westwood Hill and Sydenham Hill. Distance approx 5 kilometres.

Try to make an advance arrangement - see the gazetteer- to view the interior of St Philip the Apostle Church.

From the roundabout proceed northwards on the east side along **Sydenham Hill**, passing **Grange Court (43)** and **nos 14, 16 & 18 (44)**. Turn right along Wells Park Road, passing **nos 151/159 (29A)**, and enter **Sydenham Wells Park (55)**. Walk

34 - SYDENHAM

diagonally through the Park, passing the ponds and emerging onto **Longton Avenue (28)**, then turn left. Turn left into **Taylors Lane**, noting **nos 69/71 (46)**. On reaching Wells Park Road, turn right for **St Philip the Apostle Church (47)** - try to see the interior. Retrace steps along Wells Park Road up to Sydenham Hill, then turn right.

Continue along Sydenham Hill, passing **Highfield (48)**, **The Cedars (49)** and **Sydenham Hill House (50)**. Take the footpath on the right to **Lammas Green (51)**, then return to Sydenham Hill and continue past **Castlebar (52)** to the roundabout. Cross the road, and bear left past **nos 133 & 1435 (53)** and **The Pantiles (54)**. Turn right along **Cox's Walk (55)** down to **Cox's Walk footbridge**, then retrace steps up to Sydenham Hill. Turn right, with **Sydenham Hill Wood (56)** on your right.

(An alternative, if you have time, would be to descend from the footbridge to the old track-bed and walk along to the tunnel-mouth, then take the footpath on the right up and over the tunnel-mouth to the entrance in Crescent Woood Road, then turn left for Sydenham Hill.)

Continue along Sydenham Hill, passing the junction with Crescent Wood Road, and look at **Beltwood (57)** over the hedge. On reaching **Dulwich Wood House (58)**, turn right into **Crescent Wood Road (59)**, noting **nos 1** and **3** to the left, and **Six Pillars** and **nos 2 & 4** to the right.

Return to Sydenham Hill and turn right, passing **no 17 (63)** and **no 11 (64)**, and you are soon back at the roundabout at the junction with Westwood Hill.

WALK no 4 (including Kirkdale, the Sydenham Park Estate, Round Hill). Distance approx 4 kilometres.

On leaving **Sydenham Station (1)**, walk down Station Approach to Silverdale, turn right to Sydenham Road, then right again. Pass **The Greyhound (23)** and **Cobb's Corner (24)** and continue along the east side of Kirkdale. Turn right into **Peak Hill Avenue (65)** and into **Peak Hill (66)**, returning to Kirkdale each time. On reaching the **Church of the Resurrection (67)**, note **Park Hall (68)** opposite and turn right along **Sydenham Park (69)**. At the junction turn left along **Sydenham Park Road (70)**. Take a look at **Albion Villas Road (72)**, a cul-de-sac to the right.

On reaching **Dartmouth Road (73)**, cross to Round Hill opposite, noting **Round Hill Lodge (73)** on the corner. Going up Round Hill, note **Courtside (73)** to the left, then **St Antholin's spire (75)** in a small housing estate to the right. At the end of Round Hill, bear left to **Baxter Field (76)**, take the path across, and bear left up to **Charlecote Grove (77B)**.

At the end is **Kirkdale (77)**. Kirkdale has numerous places of interest, and it is best to turn right and walk up, noting **Eliot Lodge (77A)** en route, to the roundabout at the junction with Sydenham Hill and Eliot Bank. Then proceed downhill, block by block **(77A-D)**, as in the Gazetteer, until you are back at Westwood Hill and Sydenham Station.

CRYSTAL PALACE

Introduction

The Crystal Palace was the greatest leisure attraction the country had ever known. It is difficult to appreciate now the influence it had at the time, or to exaggerate the impact it had on surrounding areas, especially Sydenham.

The Great Exhibition of 1851

Prince Albert, as President of the Royal Society of Arts, together with Henry Cole, one of the Society's most prominent members, wanted to emulate the success of the Great Exhibition in Paris of 1849. They conceived the British exhibition as an international exhibition; it was originally planned to be at Somerset House, but it was soon realised that it was not large enough. So in 1850 it was decided to build a specially designed centre in Hyde Park, and a Royal Commission was appointed, with Prince Albert as President, and the railway engineer Robert Stephenson as Chair of the Executive Committee. A design competition was organised, but all entries were rejected. Then the Illustrated London News in July 1850 published drawings of a building made of glass 'like a giant greenhouse' designed by Joseph Paxton; this was widely acclaimed and quickly adopted.

Paxton and the Palace

Joseph Paxton was born in 1803 at Wilton Bryant, near Woburn. In 1826 he was appointed Head Gardener at Chatsworth House, and in 1836 built the great Conservatory there, then the largest in the world. He laid out Princes Park Liverpool in 1842, and Birkenhead Park in 1844.

The foundations were laid in Hyde Park in August, the first iron columns erected in September, and the whole building completed in January 1851. The name 'Crystal Palace' was given to it by Punch magazine. 'The Great Exhibition of the Works of Industry of all Nations' was opened by Queen Victoria on 1st May 1851. Exhibits included the Koh-i-Noor diamond, before it was placed in the Queen's crown. There were over 6 million visitors by the time it closed on 15th October. The museums in South Kensington were partly funded by the profits of the exhibition and stocked at first with many of the exhibits.

Penge Place

Paxton (by then Sir Joseph) wanted the Palace to stay in Hyde Park, but Parliament disagreed. He then formed the Crystal Palace Company, which bought the Palace, as well as a mansion called Penge Place near Sydenham Hill, its grounds and an adjoining estate. Penge Place was the home of Leo Schuster, a director of the

Brighton Railway (which had absorbed the Croydon Railway in 1846) and also of the Crystal Palace Company; the Company decided to rebuild the Crystal Palace there.

Construction began in August 1852, and took almost two years to complete. The new Palace was opened by Queen Victoria in June 1854. The building was greatly enlarged - longer, wider and taller than the Hyde Park building; it was 487 metres long and 94 metres wide. The grounds were developed as a spectacular park, with gardens, terraces, statues and fountains in a largely symmetrical layout; the Palace itself looked down on the Upper and Lower Terraces, and below the Terraces the Grand Centre Walk descended through the grounds to the Penge Entrance.

A spur was built from the Croydon Line into the grounds, and the new Low Level Station linked to the Palace by a long glazed walkway. Later, in 1865, a new line was built from Nunhead to the High Level Station on Crystal Palace Parade, linked to the Palace by a highly ornate subway under the road.

Fountains and prehistoric animals

The grounds were laid out as an aquatic fantasy, with a multitude of fountains, fed by three great lakes acting as reservoirs. When all the fountains were in operation, there were nearly 12,000 jets of water. At the top, there were six fountains on the Lower Terrace, and below was the great Circular Fountain, with two smaller circular fountains on either side. Below this, on either side of the Grand Centre Walk, were two 'water temples', with cascades leading down to the huge Great Fountain Basins, with the jets of the main fountain in each reaching a height of 75 metres. Two much smaller fountain basins were located at either end of these great basins, and one of these is the sole survivor of the whole system of fountains.

This fantastic system of waterworks originated in the Tidal Lake, the largest reservoir, fed by an artesian well 175 metres deep. From here a pumping station, sited where the Information Centre is now, pumped water to the Intermediate Lake; from here another station just to the north pumped water to the Upper Reservoir; finally, water was pumped from here into tanks in water towers on either side of the Palace. The original tanks were found not strong enough, so two new towers 60 metres high were constructed by Isambard Kingdom Brunel in 1856.

Models of 33 prehistoric animals were erected on islands in the Tidal Lake; they were designed by Waterhouse Hawkins under the guidance of Professor Richard Owen, who was then the leading prehistory expert and had coined the name dinosaur. A fantastic dinner party for about 20 leading scientists was held in the mould for an iguanadon on New Years Eve 1853. 27 models have survived; they were as true to life as was possible at the time, but many have been found subsequently to be quite inaccurate.

Exhibitions and events

In each of its first 30 years the Palace was visited by over 2 million people. Apart from the permanent exhibitions (cultural, ethnographic, natural history, industrial), there were many temporary exhibitions, shows and conferences; these included the world's first aeronautical exhibition in 1868 and the world's largest motor show in 1903. Great music festivals and concerts, including performances of Handel's music with over 2000 singers, were promoted by the conductor August Manns and the musicologist Sir George Grove, who was secretary of the Crystal Palace Company.

Ballooning and great fireworks displays were amongst the activities in the grounds. For a few months in 1864 an experimental pneumatic railway operated between the Sydenham Gate and the Penge Entrance. An aquarium, then the largest in the world, was opened alongside the Upper Reservoir in 1872.

But by the 1880s the full fountain displays had been largely abandoned, as the supply of water was often inadequate.

Crystal Palace Football Club

In the 1890s the southern Great Fountain basin was converted to a football pitch. The cup final and international matches were played there 1895-1914. Crystal Palace Football Club was founded in 1905, and had its grounds here until 1914. The Club then used grounds at Herne Hill Stadium until 1919, and at The Nest (opposite Selhurst Station) until 1924, when they moved to their present grounds in Whitehorse Lane, Selhurst Park.

Towards the end

Financially the Crystal Palace Company was not a success. Maintenance was extremely costly, and because of the influence of the Lords Day Observance Society, the Palace was not allowed to open on Sundays. In 1866 there was a serious fire which destroyed the north wing and transept, and these were never replaced.

To raise money, much of the land on the fringes of the Park was sold in 1871 and in 1883, mainly for housing. By 1909 a third of the land had been sold, and plans were made to sell the rest of the park. In 1911 a great Festival of Empire was held in the Palace and the Park, but in the same year, when the Company was facing bankruptcy, Lord Plymouth bought it. The Lord Mayor of London then started a fund which bought it for the nation in 1913.

During the 1914-18 War the Palace and Park were closed to the public, and used by the Navy for barracks and training. From 1920 to 1924 the Palace was the Imperial War Museum, and although repaired and restored, never fully recovered its earlier glory; there were however lots of activities in the grounds, including motor racing. The south tower was used by John Logie Baird as an early television studio.

On the night of 30th November 1936 the whole building was consumed by fire, lighting up the sky for miles around. Only the two water towers survived. The site was cleared in 1937, except for the towers, which were demolished in 1941 as it was considered they were a landmark for German aircraft.

The Park postwar

In 1951 responsibility passed to the London County Council to use the site for 'the purposes of education and recreation and the furtherance of art, commerce and industry'. Building of the National Sports Centre by the LCC started in 1960, and it was opened in 1964; since 1986 it has been run by the Sports Council. From 1953 to 1972 the Park hosted important motor racing events. A large range of sports facilities are provided in the Park, which is now run by the London Borough of Bromley.

Considerable local controversy is currently being caused by a planning application for a great rectangular glass structure designed by Ian Ritchie on the Palace site, to incorporate a multiplex cinema, restaurants with panoramic views, and other leisure facilities.

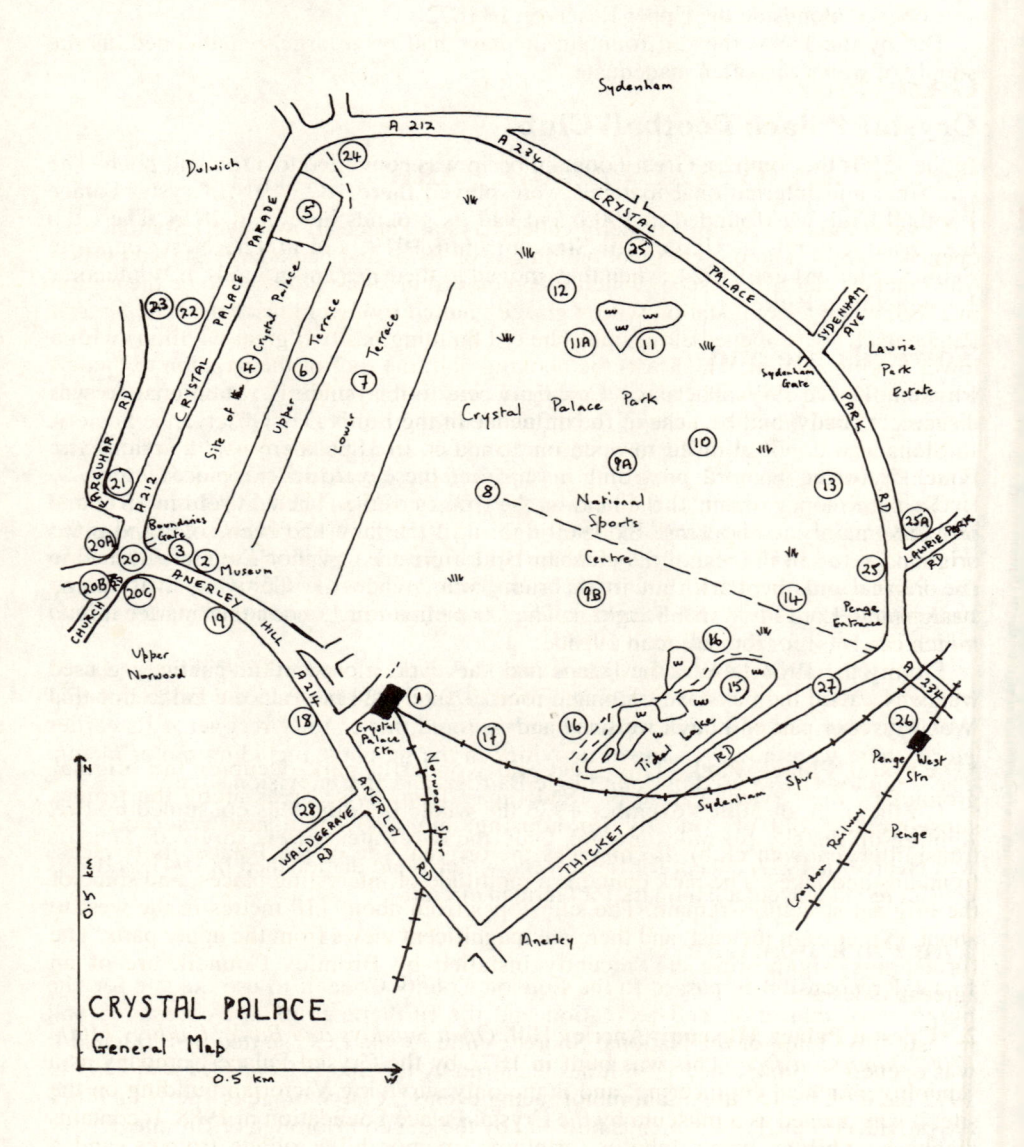

CRYSTAL PALACE
General Map

CRYSTAL PALACE

Gazetteer

Section 'A' CRYSTAL PALACE PARK

1. Crystal Palace Station, formerly called Crystal Palace (Low Level) Station, was opened in 1854. The present great building is of 1875, and had a large glazed portico (the brackets can still be seen) which was removed in 1963; it ceased to be the station in 1986, when a small station with a glazed vaulted roof (reminiscent of the Crystal Palace itself) was opened alongside. The old building has two great pavilions with a lower linking section, which was the booking-hall; the roof of the pavilion to the left was removed in 1976. There is no public access to the building, which is at present disused; it once included a chapel, a bar, and a dining-room.

Steps lead down from the new station to old covered walkways to the platforms. First, Platforms 1 and 2 providing a service from London Bridge or Victoria to Beckenham or Croydon; this line was opened in 1856. Then Platforms 3 and 4 providing a service between London Bridge and Victoria via Sydenham; this was the original line of 1854 using the Sydenham Spur from the Croydon Line, and these are the original platforms with great red brick blank arcades. To the west all trains go straight into the Gipsy Hill Tunnel, over 500 metres long, opened 1856; the tunnel mouth can be seen from the road outside.

From the station, after a few steps into the Park, a covered and largely glazed walkway called the Crystal Colonnade used to take visitors up to the Palace; of this walkway, only part of a brick wall now survives.

*****Crystal Palace Park.** This great and wonderful park occupies the original grounds of the Crystal Palace of 1854 (apart from those areas along the fringes subsequently sold off, mostly for housing, but also for a new reservoir, TV transmitter, caravan club). It embraces the original site of the Palace, its terraces, fountains and lakes. The park contains a multitude of interesting places, and some of the original structures remain. The site slopes from about 110 metres in the west to about 55 metres in the east, and there are magnificent views from the upper parts. The furnishings, signposting etc, recently installed by Bromley Council, are of an agreeable design.

2. *Crystal Palace Museum, Anerley Hill. *Open Sundays and Bank Holidays 1100-1700, admission free.* This was built in 1872 by the Crystal Palace Company as a school of practical engineering, and is the only surviving Victorian building on the site; it was opened as a museum by the Crystal Palace Foundation in 1988. It contains displays, exhibits, prints, photos, artefacts, memorabilia, objets trouvés, and a bookshop.

3. South water tower. Only the **base** remains of this water tower, constructed together with another to the north by Isambard Kingdom Brunel in 1856, when the original towers were found inadequate for the fantastic system of fountains and cascades. Both water towers, approx 60 metres high, survived the great fire of 1936, but were demolished in 1941 as they were considered a landmark for German aircraft. The south tower base adjoins the Museum, and is hard up against Anerley Hill.

By the steps opposite is an original 1851 cast iron column, repainted in the probable original colours; it was used for drainage as well as support.

The steps continue to the:

4. Site of the Crystal Palace. From south to north, first nice flower-beds, then a lawn with a headless nymph, one of the original stone figures. Beyond is some rough land, by the old south transept entrance; then you come to a modern entrance, built for the motor races which took place 1953-72, leading to a concourse down into the Park. Then you come to the old main entrance, with some brickwork and iron railings surviving, now used as a bus turning-point; there is no longer a route into the Park at this point. Here is the entrance to the High Level Station subway *(at present no public access, see Crystal Palace 21)*.

You finally come to a field with a television transmitter, of 1954; this field, to which there is no public access, is the northernmost part of the original site of the Crystal Palace.

5. Reservoir, grass covered, of Thames Water; this is a new reservoir occupying the site of the former **Upper Reservoir**, which was the uppermost of the three large reservoirs used for the fountain displays in the Park. Beyond the lane alongside is the site of Rockhills *(see Crystal Palace 24)*, now used by the Caravan Club.

The lane alongside the Caravan Club, called Rockhills Lane, leads behind the reservoir to the brick remains of an aquarium, the world's largest when opened 1872.

6. *Upper Terrace. About 475 metres long, it is lined by balustrades (restored in recent years and mostly in good condition), overlooking the Lower Terrace below. In the centre a staircase goes down to the Lower Terrace, but the route up to the Palace site has gone, though large blocks of masonry can be seen in the undergrowth. At both ends are flights of steps mostly flanked by sphinxes, and along the balustrade are a bearded and turbanned stone figure and the torso of a draped female figure. (The sphinxes are plaster casts made at the Louvre of a sphinx originally found in Tanis, Egypt.) From the Upper Terrace the views to the east are wide and magnificent.

7. *Lower Terrace. About 500 metres long, it is located between the balustrades of the Upper Terrace, which look very impressive from here, and the balustrades and grass banks (where there were steps) overlooking the National Sports Centre. The terrace is quite wide, it was originally set up as an Italian garden with six fountains. A wide flight of steps in the centre leads down to the concourse through the Sports Centre and eastwards through the Park to the Penge Entrance.

Under the terrace, at the far northern end, is a statue of Dante wearing a cloak, but headless.

8. *Bust of Paxton. This great marble bust, by William Frederick Woodington 1869, was originally on the Lower Terrace; it was installed here (just west of the site of the Great Circular Fountain) on a modern plinth in 1981. The inscription says: 'Sir Joseph

Paxton MP, 1803-1865, creator of the Crystal Palace which stood near this site 1854-1936'. In effect, the bust marks the entrance to the National Sports Centre.

9. *National Sports Centre. This is a large complex, occupying the site of the Water Temples and of the Great Fountain Basins. The modern concrete concourse through the Centre is elevated above the route of the original Grand Centre Walk.

To the north of the concourse is **The Lodge**, a hotel primarily intended for Sports Centre users, consisting of a polygonal point block of 1964, clad with vertical cedar boarding. Around are largely glazed restaurant and conference rooms in modernist style, and a staff-block with a V-shaped roof.

The buildings of the National Sports Centre, completed 1964, occupy the site of the Great Fountain Basins - the **Sports Hall (9A)** the north basin, and the **Athletics Stadium (9B)** the south basin. The Water Temples were located on either side of the concourse to the west before you reach these buildings.

The sports hall (incorporating an indoor arena and swimming-pools) has a concrete roof, supported by a central concrete triangular frame from which it is cantilevered out. Just south is the Crystal Palace Dance Studio, top-lit by white cones on the roof. Further south, the athletics stadium has two graceful semi-circular stands, added in 1977.

10. The RNVR memorial consists of a ship's bell in an open rustic timber hut; it was erected in 1931, originally on the Lower Terrace, and commemorated the use of the Park during the 1914-18 War as a naval training depot.

11. Intermediate reservoir, quite a large lake surrounded by fencing and trees, now used solely by Crystal Palace Angling Association. It was a holding reservoir for water pumped up from the tidal lake; a pumping station just to the north pumped water up to the Upper Reservoir and the water towers and tanks.

Opposite is the **maze (11A)**, the largest maze in London; it was originally developed in 1872, but fell into disuse during the last war, and was rebuilt with hornbeam hedging by Bromley Council 1988.

This north-west part of the Park is like parkland, undulating grassed areas with dense copses and wonderful trees, and has perhaps changed little since 1854.

12. *Concert platform, a startling sculptural structure designed by Ian Ritchie 1997, facing the Concert Bowl which forms a natural amphitheatre. The concrete platform is behind a water-lily pond which was an extension of the intermediate reservoir; to the rear and sides it is surrounded by a moat from the pond, and the only access to the island platform is by a drawbridge over the moat at the rear. The roof is an acoustic canopy at an inclined plane of 40 degrees; it is a great sheet of untreated Corten steel which over time oxidises into a dark brown colour. On either side are two monolithic pillars housing speakers, also of Corten steel.

13. The site of the pneumatic railway. The railway was set up in 1864 by Thomas Rammell between Sydenham Gate and Penge Entrance, running for 550 metres through a brick-lined tunnel. A vacuum was created between gates at each end of the tunnel by a large fan powered by a stationary steam engine, which in effect blew or sucked the train along the track. It operated for a few months only, and nothing now survives (although a small section of the original track-bed was excavated by the Marquis du St Empire in 1989).

14. Information Centre. From here the only remaining section of the original **Grand Centre Walk**, still flanked by double rows of plane trees, leads westwards to the National Sports Centre. Around here are some interesting structures, including: part of the head of the Hylaeosaur (this part is original, replaced by a modern plastercast replica on the island, *see 16*); a statue of Andromeda, chained to a rock with a monster at her feet; two late 19th century drinking fountains; and a K6 telephone kiosk *(see Forest Hill 25)*. Behind here is a boundary post inscribed 'Hamlet of Penge 1875' (Penge was a detached hamlet of Battersea Parish until 1899, when Penge UDC was formed; it became part of Bromley Borough in 1965). Nearby was a pumping station which pumped water from the Tidal Lake to the Intermediate Reservoir.

15. Tidal Lake, originally the Lower Reservoir, the largest of the reservoirs. It is fed by artesian wells, and when the fountains were playing, the water returned here. It is now used as a boating lake; in the western part are the dinosaur islands *(see 16)*.

16. **The dinosaur trail. The 27 models of prehistoric animals, not all dinosaurs, on and around two islands in the Tidal Lake, are surviving structures from the Crystal Palace Park of 1854. The models, originally of 33 animals, mainly of brick and iron covered by plaster, were designed by Waterhouse Hawkins with the guidance of Professor Richard Owen (who was then the leading prehistory expert); they were as true to life as was possible at that time, but many have been found subsequently to be quite inaccurate. The suggested route of the trail described below goes backwards in time, from the tertiary epoch (up to 65 million years old) to the secondary epoch (up to 245 million years old). Quite apart from the exhibits, the area is highly attractive.

Coming from the Penge Entrance, take the path to the right of the Tidal Lake. The prehistoric area of the Lake is separated by barriers from the boating area. First you pass **Gorilla**, a sculpture in black marble by David Wynne 1961.

Then you commence the dinosaur trail proper in the tertiary epoch, on a promontory which stretches into the Lake. Take the path to the left, which passes a family of megaceros (or Irish elks). Behind a wire fence you can see a megatherium (or giant sloth). Crossing a stone bridge, a clearing on the right should display models of palaeotherium and anopletherium (like tapirs), but they have recently been removed for repair (at present in a wired enclosure behind the Information Centre).

Continue to the iron bridge, which is c1985, and you enter the secondary epoch. To the left can be seen the head of a mosasaur (like a giant lizard), and above on the island to the right two pterodactyls. The path now gives fine views of four great dinosaurs on the island - the two iguanadons, a hylaeosaur *(see 14)* facing away, and a megalosaur. Continuing, on and in the water channels around another smaller island are teleosaur (like long-nosed crocodiles), plesiosaur (with long necks), ichthyosaur (dolphin-shaped), labyrinthodon (like giant toads), and dicynodon (like turtles).

Return along the path parallel with the lakeside path, and you are soon back on the iron bridge. Here to your left are the Geological Strata of the primary epoch (about 300 million years old) - they are an accurate model of Coal Measures found at Clay Cross, Derbyshire, showing seams of coal, red ironstone, and old red sandstone. Continue along the path over the stone bridge back to the beginning of the Trail.

17. Children's zoo. Apart from farmyard animals and peacocks, there is a duck-pond (with some flamingoes) which was originally the fountain for the great South Basin Pool. This is actually the sole survivor of Paxton's great system of water displays.

CRYSTAL PALACE

Gazetteer

Section 'B' THE FRINGES OF THE PARK
(See map on page 38)

18. The Paxton Arms Hotel, 52 Anerley Hill, an imposing pub, originally of the late 1850s, rebuilt as a virtual replica in 1955.

19. *Harefield, 14 Anerley Hill, a harmonious and gleaming stuccoed villa, probably of the 1830s, with a fine porch and fanlight, coach-house to the left.

20. The Boundaries. At this roundabout in Upper Norwood, the boroughs of Bromley, Southwark, Lambeth and Croydon meet, and the borough of Lewisham is only 500 metres away at the northern end of Crystal Palace Parade. Of the four corners, three are occupied by pubs, the other by the Boundaries Gate into Crystal Palace Park, erected 1988 and inscribed 'Site of Vicar's Oak' (which was a boundary oak).

White Swan (20A), 79 Westow Hill (in Lambeth), an attractive Italianate pub, probably c1850, greatly enlarged in the 1880s, of brick with plentiful stone dressings, quoins, rusticated ground floor, and a porch; the top floor was lost as a result of war damage.

Next door **77a Westow Hill**, a building of 1884, bears a plaque, sponsored by Crystal Palace Foundation and National Westminster Bank, as follows: 'Camille Pissarro 1830-1903, impressionist painter, stayed on this site 1870-71'.

> Camille Pissarro, the celebrated French impressionist painter, lived here and in Anerley from December 1870 to June 1871. He painted a number of landscapes in the Crystal Palace, Sydenham, Norwood and Dulwich areas. *(See also Sydenham 35, 55.)*

The Cambridge (20B), 2 Church Road (in Croydon), has decorative ceramic tiling on the ground floor, and an Italianate upper floor; it is of 1861, the tiling later.

Opposite, the classical upper floors of **3/13 Church Road** remain from the original Royal Crystal Palace Hotel, c1853. **The Sportsman (20C)**, 2 Anerley Hill (in Bromley), incorporates a small part (much rebuilt after war damage) of the Hotel; it is currently in the course of restoration by Regent Inns.

21. The site of Crystal Palace (High Level) Station lies below the wall along Crystal Palace Parade, and is now occupied by a health centre and houses in Bowley Lane. The station was opened in 1865, a grand terminus designed by Edward Barry; but the line closed in 1954, the station building (which fronted Farquhar Road) being demolished 1961. A great length of arcaded buttress walling, consisting of stock brick arches with red brick niches, spandrels and cornice, survives in good condition hard under the Parade; it can be readily seen from Spinney Gardens *(see 22.)*

43

The arcade leads to the **tunnel mouth** of the Paxton Tunnel, an imposing and ornate archway of white and red brick. The tunnel, about 400 metres long, emerged in what is now the Hillcrest Estate *(see Sydenham 29)*.

But the most extraordinary survivor of the station is a **subway**, also designed by Edward Barry, which gave access for firstclass passengers direct from the station to the entrance to the Great Central Transept of the Palace. The subway is an astonishing and vivid Byzantine chamber, with three parallel rows of octagonal white brick columns with flared heads of diaper patterned red and cream brickwork, interlaced with stone ribs. Holes for gas-lighting are still there in the ceiling. The vaulted roof is of remarkable strength, as it was never intended to sustain the present volume of traffic on Crystal Palace Parade directly above.

> *The subway is not at present accessible to the public. It is to be hoped that at some time in the future it can once again be a feature of the guided walks organised by Crystal Palace Foundation. These walks normally take place on the second Sunday in each month throughout the year, telephone for details 0181-778 2173.*

22. *Spinney Gardens. An energy-saving housing development c1982, with a remarkably rural atmosphere, by PCKO, a team of Polish architects led by Georges Palejowski. The houses occupy a series of linked rural courtyards, and have projecting triangular glazed porches and conservatories which act as solar collectors. There is an excellent view of the estate from Crystal Palace Parade above; to the west is Dulwich Upper Wood *(see 23)*.

The estate is on the site of the railway tracks, with the arcaded walling alongside *(see 21)*, between the former station and the tunnel mouth, in front of which is a postwar miniature locomotive, part of the architects' concept and symbolising the former railway use of the site.

23. Dulwich Upper Wood. This woodland on a slope was part of the Great North Wood, though c1870 it became part of the gardens of houses in Farquhar Road (now demolished). The wood incorporates front garden walling and basements of some of the Farquhar Road houses. It is now a nature reserve, laid out 1985. At the top, just below Spinney Gardens, is Railway Pond, with a variety of aquatic plants.

24. The site of Rockhills. Rockhills was a large mansion (built early 19th century, demolished 1960) adjoining Penge Place, where Paxton lived during the construction of the Crystal Palace and until his death in 1865. Some old gateposts and a lengthy stretch of old walling remains. The site of Rockhills and its grounds has since c1989 been used by the Caravan Club; it is the largest camping ground in London.

25. *Crystal Palace Park Road sweeps in a graceful bow downhill alongside the Park. It is particularly noteworthy for a sequence on the south side of fantastic large red brick mansions, built on land sold by the Crystal Palace Estate in 1871 and mostly designed in the 1870s, some in the early 1880s, by John Norton, the Estate's architect, who lived in the now demolished no 55. (The houses at the top on the north side are more conventional stock brick mansions of the early 1880s.)

Note, in particular, going downhill on the south side:

Nos 75/77, just beyond the Rockhills site, imposing, with a Gothic doorway and a mock-Tudor jetty on two levels.

No 69, an incredible extravaganza, c1873, with a wonderful Gothic porch and fine Gothic windows, including staggered windows to the side and a bow window.

No 67, quite lavish, with a mix of Gothic and Tudor motifs, fanciful bargeboarding and fine brickwork.

Arran House, no 65, very fanciful and stylistically eccentric, with a recessed round-headed porch with Gothic capitals, a Venetian window above, and pargetting.

No 61, another extravaganza in a mix of styles, of 1882, with a terracotta medallion of a female head, and strange stone vases recessed into the brickwork.

Faircroft, no 59, a very fanciful Gothic house, with an extended wooden porch and canopy, fine brickwork, and amazing bargeboarding.

No 57, a fantasy, of 1882, with fine porches, Gothic and Tudor motifs.

Nos 35/49 form a group of splendid houses with similar features, such as ornamental porches at the head of great staircases, and half-timbered gables.

The Vale Gate occupies the site of a house c1880 demolished 1977; the front gateposts and railings have been restored.

Between no 25 and no 15 there is a gap in the sequence of mansions on the south side. On the opposite side of the road, however, note: **no 38**, a converted mid 19th century coach-house, stuccoed, formerly for a large house, now demolished; also, **Park Court (25A)**, three quadrants of long low blocks of flats, of brick painted white, by Sir Frederick Gibberd 1936.

Back on the south side, **nos 5/15** form a group of stately Gothic houses, with nice porches and fine large Gothic windows.

Nos 1/3, with Dutch gables, but less extravagantly designed than the other houses.

26. *Penge West Station was opened as Penge Station on the Croydon Line 1839, but closed 1841; it re-opened 1863 as Penge Bridges Station, and was renamed Penge West 1923. The present low stock brick building is of the second station of 1863, but the white building to the left, **1/2 Station Cottages**, is the original keeper's lodge for the first station of 1839 - note the unusual window pattern.

The railway bridge nearby in Penge High Street is modern; a short way to the west is a great brick bridge of 1854 of the Sydenham Spur from the Croydon Line into Crystal Palace (Low Level) Station.

27. *Thicket Road, beyond the Penge Entrance into the Park, continues on the west side the sequence of large red brick mansions in Crystal Palace Park Road, designed in the 1870s and early 1880s by John Norton *(see 25)*.

No 81 is the remaining house of a pair with Dutch gables like 1/3 Crystal Palace Park Road round the corner.

Nos 75/79 are like 5/9 Crystal Palace Park Road.

Opposite is a long sequence of large Italianate pairs c1865.

Further along Thicket Road is a sharply skewed railway bridge with an ornamental parapet, on the Sydenham Spur of 1854.

28. *New Church Court, Waldegrave Road. Originally the Swedenborgian Church, or New Church, of 1883, an early example of a concrete church, made from red-coloured Portland cement. The design is very Gothic - above a doubled arched Gothic entrance is a steep Gothic gable framing a large rose window, and there are lots of lancet windows and other interesting decorative details. It was converted to residential flats c1993.

FOREST HILL

Introduction

The development of Forest Hill began in the 1780s in the area we now know as Honor Oak, on the northern part of the series of hilly ridges, mostly over 100 metres high, which stretches from Oak of Honor Hill to Sydenham Hill and Crystal Palace Parade. Part of this early development, towards the southern end of Honor Oak Road, was in fact an encroachment on Sydenham Common.

Forest Hill was subsequently influenced by the same series of events which shaped the development of Sydenham to the south - the enclosure of the Common in 1810-19, the opening of the railway in 1839 (facilitated by the opening of the Croydon Canal in 1809), and the coming of the Crystal Palace in 1854.

Honor Oak

Honor Oak Road was originally named Forest Hill. One house, Hill House, survives in part from the early encroachment on the Common; other houses nearby date from the years following the enclosure of the Common. Several houses in Honor Oak Rise, and the core of some houses in the northern part of Honor Oak Road are also from that period.

Honor Oak now covers a wide area, embracing not only the development on the ridge, with its fantastic views, but also the steep woodland of Oak of Honor Hill, the adjoining cemetery, the great waterworks to the west, and the vast Honor Oak Estate of the 1930s to the north.

The coming of the Railway

The London & Croydon Railway acquired the Croydon Canal in 1836. The railway line, which opened in 1839, followed a direct route through the area. The canal bed had followed a circuitous route to avoid the hillier contours around Honor Oak, and consequently only limited use was made of it until the stretch to the south of Forest Hill Station was reached.

The arrival of the railway in 1839 led to quite rapid building expansion in the area. The station, originally called Dartmouth Arms after a canal-side pub, was renamed Forest Hill in 1845, and this is an indication that the name of Forest Hill was being used to cover a much larger area than before.

By the 1860s that part of Forest Hill to the east of Honor Oak had become a railway suburb. New buildings appeared in and around London Road, Dartmouth Road, Perry Vale (absorbing the old hamlet of Perry Slough), and the western part of Stanstead Road. The developments included the Dartmouth Park Estate, between Waldram Park Road and Perry Vale, mainly larger houses (a number of which have survived) as well as the parish church of Christ Church; and West Kent Park, between Brockley Rise and the railway, smaller houses (few of which have survived). To the east of Brockley Rise, the estate of Brockley Hill Park laid out by the Conservative Land Society consisted initially of quite large houses, but was slower to develop.

The opening of the Crystal Palace added to the growth of Honor Oak, and of that part of Forest Hill which adjoins Sydenham on the west side of the railway.

Horniman Museum

Honor Oak Road dips down to London Road, then Eliot Bank and Sydenham Rise ascend steeply up to the ridge of Sydenham Hill. In the valley between is the Horniman Museum, built 1901 by Harrison Townsend, one of the most exciting buildings of its time in London. It was built to accommodate the private collection - in the fields of natural history, music and ethnography - of the tea merchant Frederick Horniman, who had lived in a house on the site. The museum building and collection were then donated to the London County Council.

Few museums anywhere have such a broad coverage of the world's natural and cultural heritage. The museum is noted for its special exhibitions, and for its educational work. The interior layout of the Museum will be transformed by the 'Horniman 2001' development scheme, with construction due to commence late 1999, for completion late 2001.

Horniman Gardens, largely the former grounds of Horniman's house Surrey Mount, is full of interest too, with its beautiful water garden, fine views, conservatory, sundials and totem-pole. Alongside the Museum is CUE (Centre for Understanding the Environment), a sensational modern building, energy-saving and environmentally sensitive.

Self-build

Forest Hill contains, in Walter's Way and Segal Close, some of the most interesting 'social self-build' schemes in London, based on a concept of the architect Walter Segal and supervised by Jon Broome of Architype. Segal pioneered this revolutionary lightweight self-build system, using a simple timber structure. Social self-build was initiated by Lewisham Council in 1978, and these schemes mark the summit of Segal's career, though some were not realised until after his death in 1985.

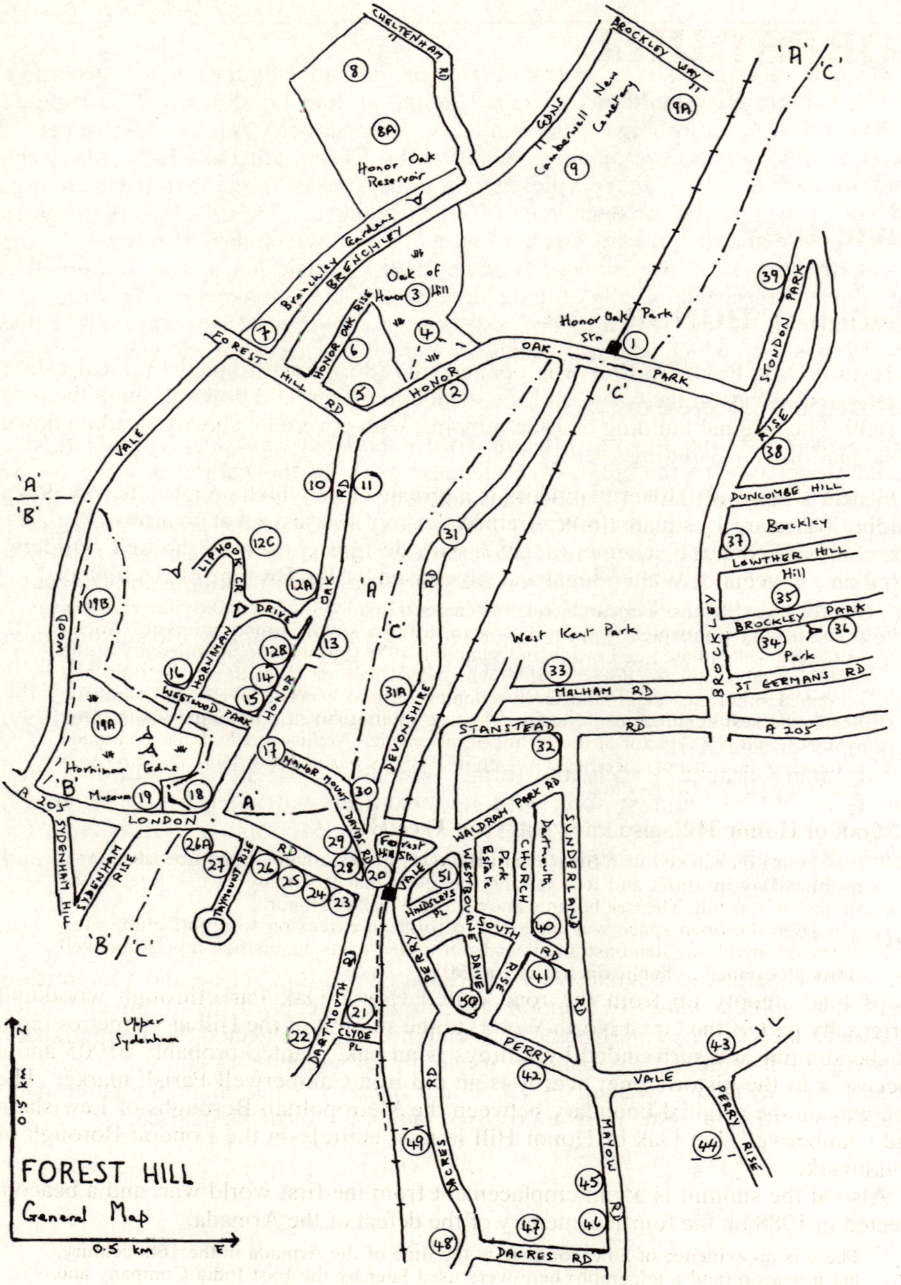
FOREST HILL
General Map
0.5 km
N
E
CHELTENHAM RD
BROCKLEY WAY
Camberwell New Cemetery
Honor Oak Reservoir
Brenchley Gardens
BRENCHLEY GDNS
Oak of Honor Hill
HONOR OAK RISE
Honor Oak Park Stn
HONOR OAK PARK
FOREST HILL RD
HONOR OAK RD
VALE
WOOD VALE
LIPHOOK CR
HORNIMAN DRIVE
WESTWOOD PARK
Horniman Gdns
Museum
LONDON RD
A 205
SYDENHAM HILL
SYDENHAM RISE
TAYMOUNT RISE
HONOR MOUNT
DAVIDS RD
Forest Hill Sta
DEVONSHIRE RD
DARTMOUTH RD
CLYDE PL
Upper Sydenham
PERRY VALE
HINDSLEYS PL
WESTBOURNE DRIVE
Park Estate
CHURCH RISE
Dartmouth
SUNDERLAND RD
SOUTH RD
WALDRAM PARK RD
STANSTEAD RD
MALHAM RD
West Kent Park
BROCKLEY RISE
STONDON PARK
DUNCOMBE HILL
Brockley
LOWTHER HILL
Hill
BROCKLEY PARK
Park
ST GERMANS RD
PERRY RISE
MAYOW RD
DACRES RD
'A'
'B'
'C'
1
2
3
4
5
6
7
8
8A
9
9A
10
11
12A
12B
12C
13
14
15
16
17
18
19
19A
19B
20
21
22
23
24
25
26
26A
27
28
29
30
31
31A
32
33
34
35
36
37
38
39
40
41
42
43
44
45
46
47
48
49
50
51

FOREST HILL

Gazetteer

Section 'A' HONOR OAK

1. Honor Oak Park Station was opened in 1886, partly funded by local estate developers. It was on the Croydon Line, which had been laid down through the area in 1839. The original building of 1886 remains, with covered walkways leading down to the platforms in a cutting.

2. Walter's Way, off Honor Oak Park, is a private close which wiggles its way down a slope. There are 13 square timber-framed flat-roof houses, set at a variety of angles. It is a social self-build scheme, of 1987, with designs chosen by the 'self-builders', based on a concept of Walter Segal and supervised by Jon Broome of Architype.

> Walter Segal, a Swiss-born architect who came to London in the 1930s, pioneered this revolutionary lightweight self-build system, using a simple timber structure. Social self-build was initiated by Lewisham Council in 1978 (through the intermediary of the architectural writer Nicholas Taylor, who was Chair of Housing at the time and produced small gap-sites), and these schemes were to become, even posthumously, Segal's highest achievement. Jon Broome was joint architect with Segal for the first schemes, and is a director of the architectural practice Architype which has continued to develop the concept since Segal's death in 1985. (*See also Forest Hill 35, Sydenham 28B, Catford 58, Grove Park 7.*)

3. *Oak of Honor Hill, also known as **One Tree Hill**.

> Elizabeth I picknicked with Sir Richard Bulkeley of Beaumaris in the Lewisham area on May Day in 1602, and it is reliably believed that it was by an oak tree on the summit of this hill. The tree became known as the Oak of Honor.
> In 1896 the open space was enclosed to form an extension to a golf club, but a campaign involving demonstrations and rioting led to its acquisition by Camberwell Borough Council as public open space in 1905.

Steps lead steeply up from the road called Honor Oak Park through woodland (originally part of the Great North Wood).to the summit of the Hill at 90 metres high. At the summit and surrounded by railings is an oak, planted probably c1905 and a successor to the historic one; nearby is an old iron Camberwell Parish marker. The tree was on the original boundary between the Metropolitan Boroughs of Lewisham and Camberwell, but Oak of Honor Hill is now entirely in the London Borough of Southwark.

Also at the summit is a gun emplacement from the first world war, and a beacon, erected in 1988 on the fourth centenary of the defeat of the Armada.

> There is no evidence of a beacon here at the time of the Armada in the 16th century, but a beacon (and a telegraph) here were used later by the East India Company and during the Napoleonic wars.

To the north the hill drops through woodland down to Brenchley Gardens (*see 7*).

4. *St Augustines Church is set half way up Oak of Honor Hill; this is a wonderful location, and the church looks good from afar, but in a closer view the detail does not measure up to the setting. It is a Gothic ragstone church, heavy and solid, of 1873 by William Oakley; the square battlemented tower was added in 1887, the Lady Chapel south of the chancel in 1894, and the north aisle enlarged in 1900. A row of circular windows forms a clerestory on both sides. Both transepts have triplets of lancets and a circular window above. Note the figure of St Augustine over the entrance. The church is surrounded by railings and fencing, and it is difficult to get a close look from anywhere except at the south-west entrance gates.

The ***interior** *(the church is normally open 1000-1100 Saturdays, otherwise contact the Vicarage, 8 Hengrave Road, 0181-699 1535)* has an imposing nave, with transepts and Gothic arcades. Original stained glass by Heaton, Butler & Bayne survives in the west window (featuring St Augustine) and the adjacent south nave window. The chancel with its apsed sanctuary contains a fine Gothic reredos of 1889 by Vincent Grose extending to the sedilia and credence on either side and forming a striking unified composition. In the south transept is a wooden panel of the Virgin Mary which was on the high altar. The stone pulpit (with a figure of St John) and the stone font are both modern in concept and have a fine though unusual design. Note along the nave the interesting carved corbels supporting the roof timbers. The Lady Chapel is attractive and intimate, with a fine wooden roof.

5. Convent of the Sacred Heart, a complex of adjoining buildings comprising two older houses and a modern school.

To the left is the **Convent**, originally an early 19th century house called Woodville Hall, with a bowed middle section; the right-hand part has been demolished to form a link with the school. In front is a statue of St Francisca Xaveria Cabrini, of 1948, a replica of a statue in St Peter's Rome.

Projecting forward from the convent is **St Francisca Cabrini School**, of 1933, large and wide, with a lively and colourful frieze incorporating a figure of Christ above the entrance door.

Adjoining is **Oaklands**, 194 Honor Oak Park, a large house of 1856, with fine round-headed windows, a tall bow window to the right, and a balustraded tower above the entrance.

Opposite, note an old classical pedimented gateway in a high wall; this led to Observatory House, a house of 1856 (with an observatory), demolished in the early 20th century.

6. *Honor Oak Rise, a highly attractive rural winding lane. The older houses are all on the east side:

Cabrini House, no 2, a large early 19th century house, with a tall bow window and a Doric porch, much altered. This building belongs to the Convent *(see 5)*.

Woodville Priory, no 14, early 19th century, with a prominent full height bow.

Nos 30/32, a fine mid 19th century Italianate pair.

Nos 34/36 and **38/40**, two large mid 19th century linked classical pairs, with Venetian windows (except on no 34).

7. Brenchley Gardens is a pleasant linear park, with an informal and irregular layout. Originally opened 1928, it now incorporates the old track-bed of the Crystal Palace High Level Railway which closed 1954. *See also Crystal Palace 21; Sydenham 29, 56; Forest Hill 19A.*. The neat rockery at the southern end was made when the track-bed was added. The track-bed forms an attractive glade, initially alongside the old park, then continuing beyond, passing on the left the Honor Oak Reservoir with the Valve House in the middle *(see 8)*; in the distance you can see the tall buildings of Central London.

8. *Honor Oak Pumping Station, of Thames Water, entrance off Cheltenham Road. A fantastic and splendid building of 1901, inscribed 'Southwark & Vauxhall Water Company', with an impressive tower topped by a fancy French chateau roof. The tower is over the original well, 100 metres deep and still in use.

In front is ***Honor Oak Reservoir (8A)**, the largest ever brick-lined underground reservoir when completed in 1909, and still probably the largest in Europe. The roof is grassed over and looks impressive; it is now used as a golf course. In the middle is the **Valve House**, a classical red brick structure of 1909, best viewed from Brenchley Gardens *(see 7)*.

9. Camberwell New Cemetery, founded 1927. The entrance off Brenchley Gardens leads to a grand building of 1930 by Sir Aston Webb; a central tower, with flying buttresses round an octagonal top stage, surmounts an archway, with chapels on either side. A separate entrance off Brockley Way leads to **Honor Oak Crematorium (9A)**, a modern brick building with a Venetian campanile, of 1939. The cemetery has no special landscape interest.

***Honor Oak Road.** This road was the original Forest Hill, laid out in the 1780s. The road retains a strong appeal, with a mix of early, mid and late 19th century houses, and postwar developments which are mostly in a sympathetic style. The road winds gently along the shoulder of a ridge, with higher ground to the west and quite fantastic views to the east.

10. Fairlawn School, Honor Oak Road. A school of 1957 designed by Peter Moro. Looking from the road, a line of projecting glazed infant school classrooms recedes from left to right, all linked by a long low block at the rear. Behind and running parallel is the Hall, and at right angles to this going westwards the junior school, a taller slab. In front, to the right, a separate classroom on columns projecting into the playground was added in 1966, and to the left a separate classroom added in 1989, both additions being in similar postwar modernist style. It is a very imaginative design, taking advantage of the fine location on a slope with fine views; it is however difficult to appreciate from the road.

Adjoining the school, **18 Honor Oak Road** was (in part) the lodge of an early 19th century house called The Manor.

11. 39 Honor Oak Road. The tall stuccoed section in the centre of this long block is basically an early 19th century house once called Forest Hill House.

Nearby, **53 Honor Oak Road** includes a tall central section, which is basically early 19th century.

12. The site of Tewkesbury Lodge. Tewkesbury Lodge was a large mansion facing Honor Oak Road, built in 1855, demolished c1930. Horniman Drive and Liphook Crescent were subsequently laid down in the grounds.

There are some interesting survivals from the grounds and the area around:

Hamilton Lodge (12A) was built c1900 by the owner Charles Bayer for his son at the northern edge of the estate. It is a large and handsome red brick house in arts & crafts style, with a rounded projecting corner.

Alongside, a lane (normally closed) leads up to the grassed top of an old reservoir; it was constructed 1887, but has not been in use since the early 20th century.

Havelock House (12B) was built c1900 by Charles Bayer for his daughter at the southern edge of the estate. It is a harmonious and handsome house in Queen Anne style, with a semi-circular porch and four fine dormers.

A **folly tower (12C)**, now in the garden of 23 Liphook Crescent, was erected c1880 in the grounds at the rear of Tewkesbury Lodge. It is quite difficult to see, and the only view from the road is between no 23 and a neighbouring house. It is octagonal, of ragstone with strong stone dressings, two storeys high with a belvedere on the roof, accessed by a spiral staircase.

From the roads around this part of Liphook Crescent, there are fantastic views to the west and over Central London.

13. Belmont, 147 Honor Oak Road, is a large rambling house of 1895 with gables, rustic porch, nice brickwork, and a hall with a cupola.

14. *Ashberry Cottage, 62 Honor Oak Road, is a highly attractive house, of the 1820s. Great rusticated and stuccoed bows through two storeys on either side of the entrance are the dominant feature, and the floor above is of brick with handsome window-cases.

A plaque says: 'Here lived William Duke of Clarence later King William IV and Mrs Dorothea Jordan actress'. However, this is very doubtful, as the house was not built until after their relationship ceased in 1811.

15. *Hill House, 64 Honor Oak Road, is in part the oldest house in the street. The plain brick part to the left with its Doric porch is c1796; the part to the right with Italianate window-cases was added c1843. Round the corner is:

2 Westwood Park, formerly called The White House, a large stuccoed house, probably c1815, and possibly a rebuild incorporating an earlier smaller house. It is difficult to see properly behind fencing, railings and trees. It has a Doric porch on the lane to the left, which leads to the stuccoed **Coach House**, originally built for The White House.

16. Horniman School, Horniman Drive, designed by Michael Manser 1972. The school is tiered down a steep hillside away from the road (and therefore difficult to appreciate from the road). It is clad in russet ribbed plastic sheets, and largely top-lit through small white cones.

17. Manor Mount has on both sides groups of interesting houses before the road bends and descends to the railway.

On the north side, first **175 Honor Oak Road**, mid 19th century, with a rustic porch, fantastic bargeboarding, Tudor and Gothic windows; adjacent is a late 19th century cottage orné with decorated bargeboards. Then follows a series of large mid 19th century pairs.

On the south side, **no 2**, large, stuccoed, mid 19th century, has a Lewisham Council plaque: 'Dietrich Bonhoeffer 1906-1945 theologian and pastor lived here 1933-35'. *See also Forest Hill 50.*

> Bonhoeffer was pastor of the German Evangelical Church in Dacres Road *(see 50)*, and this house was both the manse and a German school. On his return to Germany he became actively involved in the resistance to the Nazis. He was arrested in 1943, and executed in April 1945, a few weeks before the end of the war.

Nos 4/6, large, stuccoed, mid 19th century, was from 1875 to 1917 the forerunner of Sydenham School *(see Sydenham 74)*; the extension to the right is c1890.

No 8 is a distinctive red brick arts & crafts house of 1883, with a Gothic porch and tile-hung gables, built by Edward Mountford as the Vicarage for St Pauls Church, Waldenshaw Road (destroyed 1944).

Nos 10/18 are strange Gothic stuccoed houses with Gothic porches and windows, late 19th century.

18. 74/82 Honor Oak Road form an impressive classical group near the bottom of the hill on the west side. Going downhill:

No 74 is a detached house c1840.

No 76 is a detached house c1842. The modern house alongside is an extension to an old coach-house.

Nos 78/80 are a handsome pair of the late 1840s, with stuccoed and rusticated ground floor and porches with fluted Ionic columns.

No 82 is detached with a strong porch, c1854.

FOREST HILL

Gazetteer

Section 'B' HORNIMAN MUSEUM & GARDENS

19. **Horniman Museum. Built by Harrison Townsend for the tea merchant Frederick Horniman in 1901. It is one of the boldest and most striking buildings of its time in London. The facade of the original building, and later buildings alongside, is complex but exciting. The two original barrel-vaulted halls, the North Hall at a higher level than the South Hall, can be seen clearly from Eliot Bank and from Sydenham Rise opposite.

> On the front is a Greater London Council blue plaque: 'The Horniman Museum & Gardens were given to the people of London in 1901 by Frederick John Horniman who lived near the site'.
>
> Frederick Horniman (1835-1906) was an enthusiastic collector in the fields of natural history, music and ethnography during his extensive travels. He was the son of John Horniman, who started the tea company c1844 and was the first merchant to sell tea in packets. Frederick Horniman moved from his family home at Coombe Cliff, Croydon, to the Forest Hill area c1860, and then c1888 to Surrey House, on the Museum site. Here his collection was regularly on view to the public. As the collection grew he moved to Surrey Mount, which stood on the highest point in the present Horniman Gardens, retaining Surrey House for his collection. In 1898 he decided to demolish Surrey House, commissioning Harrison Townsend to create a purpose built museum on the site, which on completion in 1901 was donated to the London County Council.
>
> Few museums anywhere have such a broad coverage of the world's natural and cultural heritage. The museum is noted for its special exhibitions, and for its educational work.

The facade is dominated by a great and unique stone clock tower. At the top it is circular with four round turrets, at the bottom it is square with rounded corners. The round turrets, which have intricate carving in low relief, lead down through a circular cornice to four bold clockfaces; the tower then becomes a long blank expanse of stone with rounded corners until you reach the small windows at the level of the original entrance.

The main part of the building (fronting the South Hall inside) is to the left of the tower. Under a dominant curved gable is the inscription 'The Horniman Free Museum', below that a row of tiny pilasters with leafy capitals, and below that a large wall mosaic by Anning Bell, entitled 'Humanity in the House of Circumstance', an allegorical representation of intellectual, spiritual and cultural experiences between birth and death.

Further left is a smaller extension of 1911, in similar style (fronting the Emslie Horniman Gallery). Next left is at present the Education Centre, a small brick building of 1969; this will be replaced by a new building designed by Allies & Morrison as part of 'Horniman 2001' *(see below)*. Next left is CUE *(see below)*.

The original entrance is to the left of the tower, accessed by a grand staircase, with round piers and white mosaic pavements. To the left of the staircase is a bronze bowl, originally a fountain, and nearby is the foundation stone of 1898. This entrance will become a subsidiary entrance under the 'Horniman 2001' proposals.

The Museum. *The Museum is open Mondays to Saturdays 1030-1730, Sundays 1400-1730. Admission free. Telephone 0181-699 1872.*

The interior layout of the Museum will be transformed by the **'Horniman 2001'** development scheme, designed by Allies & Morrison, construction due to commence late 1999, for completion late 2001. Under this scheme, the new main entrance will be on the west side of the Museum, giving access from the Gardens behind CUE to an orientation space which will act as a focal point for access to the other galleries.

The present entrance, which is the original entrance, leads directly into the South Hall, of 1901, occupied by African Worlds, Britain's first permanent gallery of African art and culture. It is an exciting display, including an Egyptian mummy 2300 years old, voodou altars, Benin plaques, as well as works of art on African themes.

At the end of the gallery is a small lobby. Turn left up the stairs for the Music Room, of 1933, containing musical instruments from many parts of the world. Past the staircase are the cafe; the Emslie Horniman Gallery, of 1911; and the entrance to CUE *(see below)*. Continue straight ahead from the lobby to the Living Waters Aquarium, which includes an imaginative journey from the mouth of a river up to the source.

At the end of the aquarium, at second floor level, turn left into the North Hall, of 1901, containing the natural history display, the main exhibit being a great walrus, and part of the ethnographic collection. On the balcony of the North Hall is the Apostle Clock, thought to have been made in Germany in the mid 19th century.

Under 'Horniman 2001', the North Hall houses the natural history collection, the South Hall African Worlds, and the Emslie Horniman Gallery the remainder of the ethnographic collection. The new building will house a greatly enlarged Music Room, as well as the Education Centre, cafe, shop etc. During the construction period, there will at times inevitably be disruption to the displays.

The entrance to *CUE (Centre for Understanding the Environment) is at first floor level, by a bridge over a pond. (Under 'Horniman 2001', there will be a new entrance on the north side.) CUE was designed by Jonathan Hines of Architype 1995; it is a sensational modern building, planned as an auditorium and exhibition area. It is clad externally in Douglas fir, internally in pine. It has a living roof of grass and wild flowers, through which project nine hollow ventilation columns. Internally, note also the ventilation holes in the six ceiling beams. The columns and the beams together provide both structure and ventilation, with computer-controlled heat and humidity levels. The roof is irrigated by a solar-powered pump which helps to keep the building cool in summer.

CUE incorporates two sundials. On the sloping wooden ceiling is the Ceiling Sundial, by Ray Ashley and John Moir; light from the sun is reflected from a small mirror, producing a small spot of light on the ceiling, which moves eastwards as the sun moves westwards, indicating solar time against a radiating scale. On the bridge into CUE is the Butterfly Sundial, designed by Edwin Russell.

In front of CUE on the main road is a ***totem pole**, with the inscription: 'this Tlingit Indian totem pole was carved by Nathan Jackson of Alaska for the American Festival of 1985 and erected by the Greater London Council 1985'.

The Horniman Conservatory. This magnificent fully glazed conservatory was built in 1894 for Frederick Horniman at his family home at Coombe Cliff, Croydon, and was moved to this site behind the Museum 1988. The decorative white painted ironwork is by Macfarlane & Co, Saracen Foundry, Glasgow. In the south wall is a stained glass sundial, designed by Roselyn Loftin 1994.

Opposite the entrance to the conservatory is ***The Pelican Group***. This group of classical statuary was executed in Coade stone by John de Vaere at Eleanor Coade's factory in Lambeth 1797. It was a pediment over the Pelican Life Insurance Office at Lombard Street until 1915, when it was taken over by the Phoenix Insurance Company. The central figure holds a standard displaying the letters PLIO beneath a pelican 'in her piety' caring for its young. In 1934 the statuary was presented to the London County Council, and erected here in 1956.

Horniman Gardens (19A). This is a large park on a sloping site. The main gate into the Gardens from London Road led to the original drive to Surrey Mount; the railings on either side of the gate were the original railings of Surrey House. In the main part of the Gardens is the Summer Garden, comprising a rose garden and a sunken garden.

The ***Water Garden*** is delightful; a series of small ponds on the hillside feed the larger pond which surrounds CUE, and there are many exotic shrubs and trees.

By the top, near the Horniman Drive entrance, is the Dutch Barn, brought from Holland by Frederick Horniman, and the Bandstand, designed by Harrison Townsend 1912. The view from here to the west is fantastic, dominated by the ziggurat blocks of Dawsons Heights 1966-72, and St Peters Church, with its landmark broach spire, funded by Frederick Horniman and built by Charles Barry Jr 1885.

A feature of the gardens is the variety of ***sundials***. On the west face of the Museum is the Vertical West Facing Sundial, designed by Ray Ashley 1994. Near the Conservatory is the Scaphe Sundial, a smooth inner bowl with a rough exterior, designed by Angela Hodgson 1994; the shadow of the rod (or gnomon) falls on an hour line on the inner bowl. Further along is the Double Polar Sundial, with the Horniman logo and the inscription 'and hours run mad, e'en as men might' (an anagram of 'The Horniman Museum and Gardens'), designed by John Moir 1997 on a Portland Stone plinth. At the highest point of the Gardens, the site of Surrey Mount, is the Analemmatic Sundial, designed by Barry Small 1994; standing on the current month, the numbered slab on which your shadow falls is the time BST. In the Sunken Garden is the Horizontal Sundial, designed by John Moir 1997. Note also the sundials in and by the entrance to CUE, and in a window of the Conservatory *(see above)*.

The **Horniman Railway Trail (19B)** takes up the western edge of Horniman Gardens. It is a pleasant walkway along the disused track-bed, between the former Lordship Lane and Honor Oak Stations, of the Crystal Palace High Level Railway, opened 1865, closed 1954. The entrance is near London Road; the trail starts on an embankment above Wood Vale, and extends well beyond the Gardens. Towards the end the trail becomes a cutting. Beyond a clearing in the woodland, you come to a railway bridge at Langton Rise; here the trail is blocked and grassed over, and you have to return to the entrance. *Open daily 0900-1600. See also Crystal Palace 21; Sydenham 29, 56; Forest Hill 7.*

FOREST HILL

Gazetteer

Section 'C' THE RAILWAY SUBURB
(See map on page 48)

20. Forest Hill Station, a modern building of the early 1970s.

> It was opened as Dartmouth Arms Station by the London & Croydon Railway in 1839, just to the south of the present station alongside the old canal route *(see Introduction)* and behind the eponymous pub *(see below)*. The station was renamed Forest Hill in 1845, in which year an engine house was built for the atmospheric railway which ran alongside the main line between New Cross Gate and Croydon. The station was rebuilt on its present site in 1884, with a grand building and a great tower, which were demolished when the new much smaller station was built in the 1970s.
>
> The atmospheric railway was based on trains drawn along by air being sucked out of a large iron pipe laid between the rails. No locomotives were used, but the front carriage carried a piston on a bar which fitted the pipe. The air was sucked out by large steam engines in engine houses situated at New Cross, Forest Hill, South Norwood and Croydon. It was a very short-lived experiment, starting in 1846 and closing by 1847.

The subway (through to Perry Vale) was constructed in 1884. From the subway entrance a footpath leads south alongside the railway line, following the line of the canal towpath, as far as the footbridge at the end of Sydenham Park. Between Clyde Place and Sydenham Park the towpath was between the canal and a reservoir.

The Dartmouth Arms, 7 Dartmouth Road, was originally a pub of 1814 on the Croydon Canal. The present building is late 19th century, and is quite attractive.

Further south is **Bird in Hand**, 35 Dartmouth Road, a building c1820, originally on the Croydon Canal. It was much altered when it became a pub c1850.

21. Foresters Hall, Clyde Place, an interesting building of 1868 with Gothic windows and a classical porch.

Just to the south, note **107/9 Dartmouth Road**, a stuccoed pair c1840.

22. *Forest Hill Library, Dartmouth Road. An astonishing Arts & Crafts building of 1900 by Alexander Hennell, of red brick with lots of terracotta. Note the octagonal cupola over the entrance, the deep terracotta frieze across the whole building of kneeling cherubs with floral swags and shields, the Venetian window under a projecting gable. Many of the windows incorporate an art nouveau style lily motif. Inside, note the huge brackets in the hall to the left, which was the original library.

The library forms part of an remarkable group of three municipal buildings on Dartmouth Road. Adjacent are:

Louise House, designed by Thomas Aldwinckle 1890, of red brick, with a Gothic doorway and a frieze of carved terracotta tiles.

Forest Hill Swimming Pools, designed by Thomas Aldwinckle 1885, a large building of red brick, with a recessed centre flanked by projecting bays, all topped by gablets with mini flying buttresses.

23. **Barclays Bank**, formerly London & South Western Bank, of 1911, occupies a prominent corner location with an oriel window overloooking the road junction.

24. **The Old Capitol Cinema**, 11-15 London Road. An extraordinary art deco cinema of 1929 designed by Stanley Beard, but disused since 1996 and becoming derelict. It is covered in white tiles, and there are lots of interesting patterns and decorative features, including blue guilloche and other friezes, winged cherubs and lions heads. An unfortunate projecting round fascia was added in 1978 when it became a bingo hall.

Outside are adjacent **K2** and **K6 red cast iron telephone kiosks**, both to a design of Sir Giles Gilbert Scott. The K2 of 1927 has all panes of glass the same size, whereas the K6 of 1935 has narrow rectangular panes of glass.

25. ***Kings Garth**, 29 London Road. The fine central Italianate part with a nice balcony was built in 1850 as a pair; the left porch has survived, but the right porch has disappeared as part of an extension called **Princes Garth**, of 1908 by the developer Arthur Dorrell *(see 26)*. The similar extension to the left is also by Dorrell of 1908.

26. **Dorrell Estate**, which extends for some distance along London Road, is named after Arthur Dorrell, who incorporated some mid 19th century houses within a development from c1900; Lewisham Council has added further buildings since they bought the estate in 1975.

Going from east to west: **67/77 London Road** is a long and bulky but rather grand block consisting of two pairs and one detached villa of the late 1840s, linked by infill c1900. The most prominent features are the protruding square bays with inset Doric columns at first floor level which were the porches of the original houses, the grand staircases leading up to them having gone. Note the elegant balconies at the rear of the original houses.

79/85 London Road is similar but not so long; it consists of one pair of the late 1840s, with an extension c1900 to the west. Behind, in Taymount Rise, is an extension c1905 and a separate large block (part called Queens Leaze and part Queens Garth) in similar style c1905.

Off Taymount Rise, accessible by a lane alongside St Pauls *(see 27)*, note **Queens Court**, a large house, probably of the late 1850s, and **Queens Court Lodge**, a fanciful cottage orné, probably of the early 1860s, with lots of bargeboarded gables.

Silverdale Lodge (26A), facing Honor Oak Road, is a large white building of the late 1840s, its central porch flanked by full height canted bays.

27. ***St Pauls**, Taymount Rise. A Gothic ragstone church of 1863, which was handsomely and innovatively converted by Paul Brookes for residential use in 1998. Note the acute Gothic doorways and arcade, the square tower and the rose window.

> It was originally a Congregational Church, but c1923 became St Lukes Church of the Spiritual Evangel. It was rebuilt as St Pauls Church 1950, replacing a church in Waldenshaw Road, built 1878, destroyed 1944 *(see also Forest Hill 17, 29)*.

28. Railway Signal, 7 Devonshire Road, now called Hobgoblin, nicely rounding the corner with Davids Road, is a pub c1862, extended in the late 19th century.

29. 1/13 Davids Road is a terrace of 1864; some houses have altered ground floors. The houses were erected in the bed of the Croydon Canal *(see Introduction)*. The raised pavement was the canal towpath, on the east side of the canal. No 13, now Kingdom Hall of Jehovahs Witnesses, was previously in use as Forest Hill Workingmens Club and as the Mission Hall for St Paul, Waldenshaw Road *(see 27)*.

30. St Johns United Reformed Church Centre, a small Gothic church with polychrome window-hoods and bargeboarded gables. It was built 1871 as the church hall for St Johns Presbyterian Church, Devonshire Road (demolished 1983).

31. Devonshire Road was developed from the 1860s. It has two **Penfolds hexagonal pillar boxes**, almost certainly of the 1870s: in the northern part, outside no 202; and in the central part, at the junction with Benson Road. Further south is:

Post Office Sorting Office (31A), no 61, an Edwardian baroque building. Note the fine frieze, pediment and royal arms above the central window, the curved parapets on either side, and the ER ciphers over side windows. In front are a **K2 red cast-iron telephone kiosk**, to the design of Sir Giles Gilbert Scott 1927 *(see 24)*, and an Edward VII letter box.

32. Railway Telegraph, 112 Stanstead Road, an imposing pub c1853, with a central bow in the distinctive projecting ground floor. It was handsomely restored in 1998.

33. Former Zion Baptist Chapel, Malham Road, a large and rather forlorn white Gothic brick building of 1878. The chapel closed 1973, and the building has been integrated into an industrial estate.

34. St William of York Church, Brockley Park, a Roman Catholic brick church of 1906, with considerable extensions of 1931 on both sides. It is classical, with deep eaves, and a fine doorcase with Byzantine columns and shell hood.

The **interior** *(contact 0181-690 4549)* is attractive, top-lit by a small square window in the centre of a fine wooden roof. The chancel is of 1986, with orientation to the north; behind the altar is a circular window with brightly coloured stained glass by Goddard & Gibbs. At the rear of the church is an arcade with Byzantine columns.

35. Segal Close is an attractive narrow close off Brockley Park, with seven timber-framed self-build houses based on the Walter Segal concept, completed 1981 *(see Forest Hill 2)*. It was the earliest of the social self-build schemes of Lewisham; one house was built by Jon Broome of Architype in 1978.

Next to the school on the other side of Brockley Park are four self-build houses of 1996. There are four more self-build houses of 1996 on the south side of Lowther Hill, almost backing onto Segal Close.

36. Brockley Park Estate, built by Lewisham Council 1980, is at the top of the hill in Brockley Park. Partly weatherboarded houses are in imaginatively grouped clusters around a large but secluded green, and there are similar houses nearby.

The road outside provides a fantastic **view** across to the ridges formed by Honor Oak Road and Sydenham Hill, with the tower of Horniman Museum in between.

37. 1/3 Lowther Hill, a fine stuccoed Italianate pair c1870, with towers at each end. Note the numerous narrow round-headed windows - pairs in the towers, triplets elsewhere.

Lowther Hill leads steeply up to Blythe Hill Fields *(see Catford 31)*. Between Lowther Hill and Duncombe Hill is a private oblong of wooded open space, with no public access.

38. The Chandos, 56 Brockley Rise, an imposing pub of 1857.

39. 22 Stondon Park bears a joint Lewisham Council / Labour Party plaque to Jim Connell, 1852-1929, 'Irish socialist and author of The Red Flag'. He was Secretary of the Workmens Legal Friendly Society, and lived here 1915-29.

40. *Christ Church, the original parish church of Forest Hill, is a large and powerful Gothic ragstone church designed by Ewan Christian 1854; the north aisle was added 1862, but the tower and the octagonal spire were not built until 1885. The spire is very tall and very handsome, of smooth stone, with pinnacles; note the two groups of steeply hooded spire windows.

The **interior** *(contact 0181-291 3434)* has lost its original impact, because an upper floor was inserted at the west end in the 1970s and the sanctuary was partitioned off c1992. However, one can still gain some idea of its original lofty and imposing size, with a very tall chancel arch and very wide Gothic arcade arches. In the north aisle is a fine stained glass window by Sir Ninian Comper 1936.

Among the many tombs in the churchyard, note: near the church entrance, to the left a red granite obelisk over 'the family grave of George and Mary Baxter' 1867 *(see Sydenham 76)*, and to the right a gravestone to the architect Alexander Hennell (1838-1915) and family; by the west wall, a memorial in the form of a pinnacle to members of the Tetley tea merchant family, from 1872.

41. Tudor House, South Road, an impressive red brick building c1870, with an ornamental Gothic porch and a gabled front; it was built as an extension to the left of Tudor Hall, a large house built 1851, demolished 1961.

Two out-buildings of Tudor Hall, both c1851, have survived to the left - **Tudor Lodge**, the original lodge; and **Hamilton Hall**, the original stable block, which was adapted for use by the Christadelphians 1907.

42. Rose Cottage, 118 Perry Vale, is a long and low late 18th century building, with 19th century additions including the porch. It is the only survivor of the old hamlet of Perry Slough.

43. Former Forest Hill Fire Station, Perry Vale, now Forest Hill Neighbourhood Office, a romantic Arts & Crafts building of 1901, with irregular canted bays, a high roof with deep eaves and six dormers, and an octagonal tower. Note the strange curly iron hooks on the dormers and at the top of the tower.

44. Ecological Self-Build House, 11 Shaws Cottages, Perry Rise. Designed and self-built by Jon Broome of Architype 1994-96 as an energy-saving development of the self-build system pioneered by Walter Segal *(see Forest Hill 2)*. A structure of tree trunks supports a turf and wild flower roof over a lofty open-plan family room; the walls are of Douglas fir clad with larch. The site was previously a disused vegetable garden. Only the top of the house is clearly visible from Shaws Cottages, which is a public footpath.

The house is usually open to the public during the Open House weekend every September.

45. 24 Mayow Road, a large multi-gabled house c1870, with rustic timber features - doorway, bargeboarding and an oriel extending into the roof. It is the sole survivor of a group of large Victorian houses along this part of Mayow Road.

46. Forest Hill School, a large school of 1956, is distinguished by its Library, a circular wooden block on pillars, with connecting walkways to the north and south sides of the square which it helps to form.

47. Dacres Estate has five brick tower blocks of 1962 along Dacres Road overlooking Mayow Park. At the west end, outside Woodfield House, is **'Pacific'**, a sculpture c1854 from Crystal Palace.

48. *Dacres Wood Nature Reserve. A grassed area on a slope leads to this very attractive Nature Reserve. There is a boardwalk across marshy land which is on the former route of the Croydon Canal and can be considered a surviving part of the canal. The paths can become quite muddy.

49. *Dietrich Bonhoeffer Church, Dacres Road, a German Lutheran church of 1959 by G. S. Agar, in pale brick with a bold but elegant round apsed chancel facing the road.

> It replaced the German Evangelical Church of 1883 bombed during the war. A Lutheran church was first established here in 1875 to serve the many Germans who had settled in the Sydenham and Forest Hill areas. Bonhoeffer was pastor here 1933-35 *(see Forest Hill 17)*, and the church was named after him at the end of the war. The church incorporates a study centre and archive which is a legacy of those who worked in the German resistance movement against the Nazis.

The ***interior** is worth seeing *(contact 0171-794 4207 or 0181-778 6477)*. It is dominated by the brilliant stained glass, by the Whitefriars Studios, of the six tall narrow windows in the chancel. In the study centre is a triptych made by German prisoners, to a design by Herbert Klingst. In the church hall at the rear is a portrait of George Bell, former Bishop of Chichester, by Hans Feibusch 1994.

A footpath to the side leads to a footbridge over the railway to Sydenham Park *(see also 20)*.

50. 101/105 Perry Vale. No 101 is a cottage orné c1840, with Gothic and Tudor motifs. Adjoining round the corner are no 103, with similar motifs, and no 105, a smaller cottage, both mid 19th century.

51. Hindsleys Place is a small cul-de-sac off Perry Vale with several mid 19th century houses. At the beginning is Serin House, c1845 with a modern rear extension, which from 1860 to 1871 was The Armoury (Sydenham Rifle Volunteer Corps). No 3 is inscribed Cooks Place, the former name of the street, and the date 1844. Nos 5, 7 and 17/19 are also of or about this date.

Opposite is **Foresters Arms**, 53 Perry Vale, a pub c1855 with fine stuccoed upper floors and a modern ground floor.

FOREST HILL

Suggested Walks

It is recommended that the suggested walks be followed in conjunction with the Gazetteer and the maps, and that the Gazetteer be consulted at each location for a detailed description. Some locations described in the Gazetteer have not been included, as they might add too much to the length of the walks.

Walk no 1 covers Section 'A', and Walk no 2 Section 'C'. Section 'B' is not covered, as the gazetteer entry for the Horniman Museum & Gardens indicates clearly how best to see the places of interest. The walks follow a more or less circular route, so can be joined at any location. Walk no 1 begins at Honor Oak Park Station and ends at Forest Hill Station. Walk no 2 begins and ends at Forest Hill Station.

WALK no 1 (including Oak of Honor Hill, Honor Oak Waterworks, and Honor Oak Road). Distance approx 4 kilometres.

Try to make an advance arrangement - see the gazetteer- to view the interior of St Augustines Church.
On leaving **Honor Oak Park Station (1)**, turn right and start ascending Honor Oak Park. After passing the entrance to the sports ground and allotments, **Oak of Honor Hill (3)** is to your right; the slope from the first gate is quite steep, so it is a good idea to wait until you reach the second gate. Note **Walter's Way (2)** to the left of the road. On reaching the second gate, follow the slope up to **St Augustines Church (4)** - try to see the interior. Continue to the top of the Hill to the boundary oak and beacon, then retrace steps back to Honor Oak Park.

After passing the **Sacred Heart Convent (5)**, turn right along **Honor Oak Rise (6)**, then return. Continue along Forest Hill Road past the road called Brenchley Gardens, and enter the park called **Brenchley Gardens (7)**. Follow the old railway track-bed until you have a good view of **Honor Oak Pumping Station (8)** and **Honor Oak Reservoir (8A)**, then return to Forest Hill Road and turn left.

Turn right down **Honor Oak Road**, passing **Fairlawn School (10)**, **Hamilton Lodge (12A)** and **Havelock House (12B)** on the right, **no 39 (11)** and **Belmont (13)** on the left. You then come to, on the right, **Ashberry Cottage (14)**, **Hill House (15)** and, round the corner, **2 Westwood Park (15)**. Cross Honor Oak Road to **Manor Mount (17)**, note the houses on both sides before the road bends, then retrace steps. Continue down Honor Oak Road, noting **nos 74/82 (18)** on the right, to the junction with London Road.

You can now turn right for **Horniman Museum (19)** and **Gardens (19A)**, though this is best left for a separate visit. Otherwise turn left for **Forest Hill Station (20)**. (For the buildings en route, see Walk no 2).

FOREST HILL - 63

WALK no 2 (including Dartmouth Road, London Road and the Dorrell Estate, Christ Church, and Perry Vale). Distance approx 4 kilometres.

Try to make an advance arrangement - see the gazetteer- to view the interior of Dietrich Bonhoeffer Church.

On leaving **Forest Hill Station (20)**, turn left along Dartmouth Road, passing the **Dartmouth Arms** and **Bird in Hand (21)**, turn left into Clyde Place for **Foresters Hall (22)**, then return. Note the three municipal buildings opposite - **Forest Hill Library**, **Louise House** and **Forest Hill Baths (23)** - then return to **Barclays Bank (24)** at the road junction by the Station, and turn left along London Road.

You pass the **Old Capitol Cinema (25)** and the telephone kiosks outside, **Kings Garth (26)**, and the buildings of the **Dorrell Estate (27)** as far as **Silverdale Lodge (27A)**. Detour up Taymount Rise for **St Pauls (28)**. Return along London Road to the junction, turn left, noting the Hobgoblin, formerly **Railway Signal (29)**, and **1/13 Davids Road (30)**. Continue on the main road as it goes under the railway bridge and becomes Waldram Park Road.

Turn right along Church Rise up to **Christ Church (41)**. Note in South Road opposite the church entrance **Tudor House (42)**, **Tudor Lodge** and **Hamilton Hall**. At the end of South Road, turn right along Sunderland Road to Perry Vale. Turn left for the **former Forest Hill Fire Station (44)**, then return on the south side of Perry Vale. Note **Rose Cottage (43)**, and turn left down Dacres Road for **Dietrich Bonhoeffer Church (50)** - try to see the interior - and **Dacres Wood Nature Reserve (49)**.

Return along Dacres Road to Perry Vale, noting **101/105 Perry Vale (51)** opposite, then turn left along the north side of Perry Vale, noting **Foresters Arms** and **Hindsleys Place (52)**. Go under the subway opposite back to Forest Hill Station.

CATFORD

Introduction

Catford is the name of an old manor dating back to the 13th century; it certainly owes its name to a ford over the River Ravensbourne, and there may well have been a colony of wild cats there.

But Catford as the name of a particular suburban district crossed by the South Circular Road is of more recent origin. It may date from no earlier than the building in 1875 of the offices of the Lewisham Board of Works (which in 1900 became the Town Hall), or from the building of the original parish church of Catford in 1887 - these were the first dates when Catford could be said to have any separate and specific identity. The earlier railway station of 1857 was called Catford Bridge Station, whereas it was the station of 1892 which was called Catford Station.

In the early 19th century

In the early 19th century the wider area of Catford included several distinct districts. Rushey Green already seemed an outlying and quite large extension of Lewisham, with a green on the road between Lewisham and Bromley. In Perry Hill, on the lane from Rushey Green via Catford Hill to Sydenham, was until c1810 Place House, the Elizabethan manor house of Sydenham (located where Creeland Grove is now); this was historically part of Sydenham, but is now generally considered part of Catford.

Between Rushey Green and Perry Hill was Catford Bridge, there by 1744, but just a bridge over the river. To the north of the bridge was the Ravensbourne Park Estate, developed from the 1820s, though relatively few houses (but including some of high quality) were built in quite a large area. To the west was Blythe Hill House, built 1842, its grounds including a hilly mound; a precinct around Blythe Hill Lane appeared in the 1860s, and much of this survives.

The southern reaches of Catford embraced the rural village of Southend.

The coming of the Railways

Catford Bridge Station on the Mid Kent Line opened in 1857, but this had no significant effect on housing growth in the area.

However, in the years following the opening of Catford Station on the Catford Loop Line in 1892, there was a massive expansion of the residential streets of Catford. In fact housing in Catford is predominantly Edwardian in character. The streets between Stanstead Road and Catford Hill were developed from the early 1890s, the vast St Germans Estate in the adjacent part of Hither Green from 1896, and the large Forster Estate to the south after 1900.

Southend

Southend was a separate village until after the first world war, when - partly because of the Bellingham Estate - it became joined up to Catford to the north. But even now it retains a separate identity and a village-like quality.

There was certainly a village here by the early 18th century, and there were two mills on the river. The Lower Mill - the mill-pond and a small part of the mill itself survive - was famous in the early 18th century for the pioneering manufacture of high quality cutlery by Ephraim and John How. The Upper Mill was further south, beyond the Meadows Estate, and no trace now survives. The Green Man and Tigers Head pubs (though not of course the present buildings) helped to make the picturesque riverside village of Southend with its large mill-ponds a popular resort.

Throughout the 19th century the affairs of Southend were very much influenced by the Forster family, who were big landowners in Lewisham and lived at The Hall, which was located where Whitefoot Lane joins Bromley Road. The old chapel was built by the family in 1824 to serve the local area, and in 1928 (after they had left the area) they donated land for the present Church of St John, which if completed would have been of enormous proportions. The architect was the eminent Sir Charles Nicholson; this and his three churches in Bellingham and Downham were built towards the end of his working life.

The railway did not reach Southend until 1892, with the opening of both Beckenham Hill and Bellingham Stations, but this had little immediate direct impact.

Bellingham and Downham

The great estates of Bellingham and Downham were built on farmland around Southend in the 1920s. They were among the 'cottage estates' of the London County Council, mainly terraced groups of houses with gardens, and few flats. Smaller extensions to the estates were built in the 1930s. Bellingham has a semi-formal layout, with roads radiating from the central Bellingham Green, whereas the much larger Downham, stretching all the way to Grove Park, is an irregular area of curving and intersecting roads.

The three churches of Sir Charles Nicholson, each with some interesting features, add special interest to the estates.

Catford today

It is difficult to generate much enthusiasm for the town centre of Catford today. It is a very busy traffic junction - the old road from Lewisham to Bromley is crossed by the South Circular Road (the crossroads dates only from 1883, when Brownhill Road was laid out); this creates a traffic island, recently developed and called Catford Island.

Reaction to the landmarks around the centre is bound to be mixed. Negative features are the depressing precinct of the Catford Centre; the unimaginative layout and disappointing buildings of Catford Island; the rather uninspired Town Hall; and the unbelievably mediocre Laurence House. But there are positive features: the great cat draped over the entrance to the Catford Centre; the stylish Eros House; imaginative detailing on Lewisham Theatre; and the exciting new St Laurence Church of 1968, to the south of the centre.

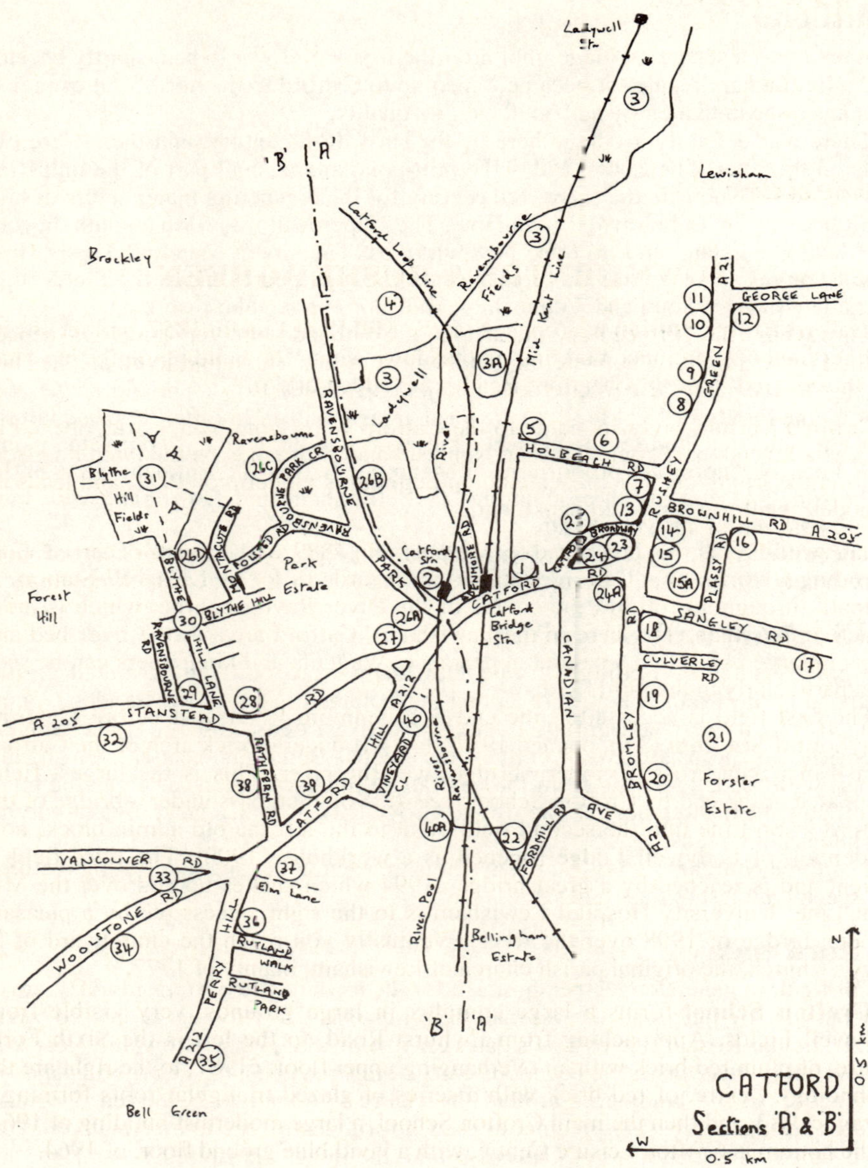
CATFORD
Sections 'A' & 'B'
Ladywell Stn
Lewisham
Brockley
Forest Hill
Bell Green
Forster Estate
Bellingham Estate
Elm Lane
Catford Loop Line
Mid Kent Line
Ravensbourne Fields
Ladywell
Ravensbourne
Blythe Hill Fields
Park Estate
Catford Stn
Catford Bridge Stn
River Ravensbourne
River Pool
HOLBEACH RD
RUSHEY GREEN
GEORGE LANE
BROWNHILL RD
A 205
A 21
PLASSY RD
SANGLEY RD
CULVERLEY RD
BROMLEY RD
CANADIAN AVE
FORDMILL RD
CATFORD RD
CATFORD HILL
A 212
VINEYARD CL
RATHFERN RD
STANSTEAD RD
RAVENSBOURNE PARK
RAVENSBOURNE PARK CR
MONTACUTE RD
BLYTHE HILL
BLYTHE HILL LANE
RAVENSBOURNE RD
VANCOUVER RD
WOOLSTONE RD
PERRY HILL
RUTLAND WALK
RUTLAND PARK
ADENMORE RD
LAWNPOOL
BROADWAY
'B' 'A'
N
W
0.5 km

CATFORD

Gazetteer

Section 'A' TOWN CENTRE & RUSHEY GREEN

1. Catford Bridge Station was opened on the Mid Kent Line in 1857, and retains its original Italianate entrance building on the 'down' side. The building on the 'up' side, and the covered steps up to Catford Road, were added c1870.

2. Catford Station gives its name to the Catford Loop Line, which was opened in 1892 as a diversionary route between Nunhead and Shortlands on the main line from Victoria to Orpington. The present station building is modern, of 1971, and leads up to modern platforms on an embankment.

3. Ladywell Fields was purchased for the public in 1889, and consists of three fields, extending from the two Catford stations northwards as far as Ladywell Station. A footpath throughout follows the course of the River Ravensbourne, which is more attractive here than elsewhere in the Lewisham / Catford area, as the river-bed and banks in large part retain a natural appearance. Wagtails and kingfishers can be seen here, particularly in the third field.

The first field is accessed at the end of Adenmore Road; just before **Catford Greyhound Stadium (3A)**, opened 1932, turn left under a brick arch of the Catford Loop Line, then cross a modern bridge over the river. This is the largest field, dominated at the end by Crofton School *(see 4)*. You then pass under a bridge of the Catford Loop Line into the second field, with to the left the old admin block, now residential, of Ladywell Lodge (opened as a workhouse 1900). The third field is ancient and is reached by a great bridge c1994 which snakes up and over the Mid Kent Line; University Hospital Lewisham is to the right, accessible by a pleasant wooden bridge of 1998 over the river. Eventually you reach the churchyard of St Mary's Church, the original parish church of Lewisham, mainly of 1777.

4. Crofton School forms a large complex in large grounds, very visible from Ladywell Fields. Approaching from Ewhurst Road, to the left is the Sixth Form Centre, of plum red brick with an overhanging upper floor, c1987; to the right are the Technology Centre, of red brick with a series of glazed triangular roofs forming a zigzag, c1987, and then the main Crofton School, a large modernist building of 1964. At the bottom is Crofton Leisure Centre, with a vivid blue ground floor, of 1964.

5. Holbeach School, an impressive red brick London School Board building of 1901, towering over the surrounding streets; the upper part is a fantastic mix of gables and turrets, with a central cupola and lots of stone detailing. The old **lodge**, now called Penfolds Manor, is striking too, with a projecting U-shaped staircase tower, topped by a strange concave tent-shaped roof.

6. Holbeach Baptist Church. A simple Gothic church, built 1883 as a Mission Hall, which then developed into St Laurence Church *(see 19)*. It became St Laurence Church Hall after 1887, and became a Baptist Church in 1954.

7. 120/124 Rushey Green. The upper floors are of 1830, but this can only be appreciated from the opposite side of the road, as they are otherwise hidden behind the modern protruding shopfronts.

8. The Rising Sun, 88 Rushey Green, now called Goose & Granite, a mock-Tudor extravaganza of 1937, with Tudor chimneypots and twisted brick door pillars.

9. The Plough & Harrow, 68 Rushey Green, was originally an old cottage c1815 which became a pub in the 1850s. The original upper floor of the cottage survives, the ground floor was rebuilt later.

10. 22 Rushey Green is basically a late 18th century house called Springfield, with no 20 to the right a mid 19th century extension.

11. Thackerays Almshouses. A strange building, with gabled ends and a central romanesque archway. The inscription reads: 'Built and endowed 1840 for 6 aged females by John Thackeray of The Priory Lewisham who died 1851'. Thackeray's monument is in St Mary's Church, Lewisham; The Priory was a large house just north of the almshouses, the last part demolished in 1932.

12. The George, 1 Rushey Green. The L-shaped building at the front, though completely restored after the war, still preserves the appearance of the pub as it was c1800; however, the porch and the rear extension are postwar additions.

Adjacent, on the south side of **George Lane**, is an interesting group of houses c1815. **Nos 2/6** are a terrace of small cottages; **nos 8/10** are a similar pair, though a modern shopfront spoils no 8. **Nos 18a, 20, 22** are a group set back behind long front gardens. **No 28** is a more substantial, originally detached house; **nos 30/32** are a pair.

13. The Catford Centre, by Owen Luder 1969-73. A large black and white cat is draped over the entrance sign outside, and arouses lively expectations. But it is a depressing complex of shops, walkways, a car park, and a housing estate called Milford Tower. It incorporates Catford Mews, an indoor market which may become more intimate when more shop units are taken.

14. Eros House, a brutalist block of 1962 by Owen Luder. A huge staircase tower is linked to a substantial nine storey concrete block, distinguished by the uneven pattern of projecting window bays, producing a jerky rhythm which shows style and panache. It may seem forbidding at first sight, but it is worthy of closer and longer scrutiny.

On the green by the road junction outside is a hand pump of the 1850s.

15. The Black Horse and Harrow, 167 Rushey Green, is a splendid pub of 1897; there has been a pub on the site since at least 1700. Among the most prominent features are great granite Ionic columns along the ground floor, arched recesses to the first floor, some grotesque carved stonework above, and a corner turret.

Behind the pub, an island site, created by the South Circular Road as it winds its way round the centre, has recently been developed and is called **Catford Island (15A)**, but the layout is unimaginative and the buildings disappointing.

16. 16/18 Brownhill Road is a corner building with a funny turret, of 1912; over the upper floor window is a stonework inscription 'Nothing without industry'. It was formerly a branch of the Bromley & Crays Co-operative Society. It is in part used as the Kingdom Hall of Jehovahs Witnesses, otherwise the building looks derelict.

17. Holy Cross Church, Sangley Road, a Roman Catholic brick church of 1904 by Francis Tasker; the sanctuary is an extension of 1924, and the front porch was added in 1949. The **interior** is in classical style *(contact 0181-698 3672)*; the orientation is to the south. Note the rose window, the rood, and the murals in the transepts.

18. ABC cinema, 1 Bromley Road. It was opened in 1913 as Central Hall Picture House, and is the only remaining cinema in the Lewisham area. There are great stuccoed Ionic columns at first floor level, but the ground floor is much less appealing.

19. *St Laurence Church, Bromley Road, an impressive octagonal church by Ralph Covell, of 1968 but still looking very modern indeed. The ground floor is of red brick, with a clerestory of stained glass, topped by a concrete roof with a concrete crown. To the north is a tent-like Lady Chapel, with a remarkable open steeple with a concrete base (containing a bell of 1897 from the previous church) and a spire of aluminium and steel above.

> This replaces a church of 1887, which was demolished in 1968 for the eventual town hall extension called Laurence House *(see 24A)*. The church had developed from a mission hall in Holbeach Road of 1883, which became Holbeach Baptist Church in 1954 *(see 6)*.

The ***interior** is quite sensational, octagonal but looking circular and with a circular sanctuary. Above the simple altar is an illuminated stained glass crucifix. The clerestory of stained glass all around was carried out by Beton of Belgium to designs of Carter Shapland. The Stations of the Cross are paintings by John Collins 1982. The interior of the Lady Chapel is very pleasing, pentagonal, lit by a small opening in the concrete ceiling; note the wood carving Martyrdom of St Laurence by Samuel Wanjau of Kenya 1975.

> *The main door is often open, allowing access to the Lady Chapel, but the actual entrance door to the church interior is normally locked. But a quite good view of the interior is possible through the glass doors on the way to the Lady Chapel. Otherwise contact 31 Bromley Road, phone 0181-698 2871.*

20. 61 Bromley Road (Priory House School), the former Sangley Farm, is a nice early 19th century villa, with a Doric porch and a later extension to the south.

21. Forster Estate, extending from Culverley Road to Newquay Road, was built between 1903 and 1914. There are long sequences, which can become monotonous, of gabled Edwardian houses. The corner houses along Bromley Road have more prominent features, proclaiming the entrance to the estate.

22. Rivers Depot, a depot of the National Rivers Authority, was built 1977 on a site between the Ravensbourne and Pool Rivers. The blank brown brick exterior looks inwards to a courtyard, and vivid red metalwork provides contrast.

23. Lewisham Theatre, known as Lewisham Concert Hall until 1984. It was built in 1932 by Bradshaw Gass & Hope, as an addition to the old Town Hall of 1875, and now forms part of an island site with the new Town Hall *(see 24)*. The theatre is a curved stone building with a cupola; it has some style, with lots of stone carvings and decorative embellishments, and gargoyles at the rear.

The *****interior** is in Art Deco style. In the vestibule is a staircase with metal railings, exotic scrollwork and distinctive lighting. The main theatre has a great iron-spanned roof, a curved proscenium arch flanked by heraldic beasts, and 10 exotic lanterns. The detailing is extraordinary and fantastic everywhere. The studio theatre, situated in the eastern curve of the building, also has exotic detailing.

24. Lewisham Town Hall. This forms part of a great oval-shaped building on an island site, with the Town Hall and Civic Suite occupying the western half, and Lewisham Theatre *(see 23)* the eastern half (apart from Town Hall Chambers, which are council offices). On the south side a section opens out to show the Town Hall of 1958-63 sweeping round from the left and the Civic Suite of 1971 to the right, with a green in front and on it **Pensive Girl**, a sculpture by Gerda Rubinstein 1994. The Civic Suite is modern and bright, but overall the Town Hall buildings appear mediocre and depressing, failing to measure up to the style of the Theatre.

Inside the **Civic Suite**, the entrance hall is lined with white marble, and the grand staircase, dominated by a large mural in Italian marble tesserae by Hans Unger and Eberhard Schulze, leads to the upper floor and the semi-circular Council Chamber.

To the south is a large Town Hall annexe of 1990, **Laurence House (24A)**, extraordinarily uninspired and boring, with a narrow glass canopy all round at the top appearing to suspend a flimsy lattice framework down to the ground.

> Laurence House occupies the site of the old St Laurence Church of 1887. The church was demolished in 1968 to make way for it, though it was not built until 22 years later. *See also 19.*

25. Catford Broadway begins from the east with two curved terraces of shops, originally of the 1880s. There is a street market on Thursdays, Fridays and Saturdays.

Further west is a terrace of 1927, and in the middle a lane leads to **Elmwood**, basically a house of 1736, but at this point hidden by a mid 19th century extension with elegant ironwork. Round the corner in Thomas Lane is the main entrance, where the core of the old building, with twin mansard roofs, can be seen, but even here it is largely hidden by 20th century extensions.

> Elmwood is in fact a survival from Rushey Green before its enclosure in 1810.

CATFORD

Gazetteer

Section 'B' BLYTHE HILL & PERRY HILL
(see map on page 66)

26. Ravensbourne Park Estate was laid out to the north of Catford Bridge from 1825, but was very slow to develop. From the early development a small stuccoed group at the beginning of Ravensbourne Park has survived, as well as an outstanding pair to the north opposite Ravensbourne Park Gardens, which was a private green for the estate. Even by the 1860s only a small number of houses had been built, and of this period three more pairs remain. The area did not become fully built up until after the First World War. Note:

7 Ravensbourne Park (26A), c1830, now part of a terrace with a modern block.

11/15 Ravensbourne Park, a pair c1830 - no 11 has a doorcase with recessed Doric fluted columns; no 15 has a bold Tuscan porch and is linked to The Cottage, which is late 19th century.

25/27 Ravensbourne Park, of the early 1870s, with some interesting decorative details.

*60/62 Ravensbourne Park (26B), c1830, an outstanding stuccoed pair, with recessed fluted Doric columns, facing Ravensbourne Park Gardens from the east and looking isolated amongst so much later housing.

57/59 Ravensbourne Park Crescent (26C), facing the Gardens from the west, originally a pair of Italianate houses c1860 with Doric porches. In 1885 no 57 was transformed in an extraordinary way - it was extended to the left, given three dramatic three-storey bows, and a grand staircase leading up to the Doric porch to which rusticated square pillars were added. In the 1970s it was extended upwards in an unsympathetic way, with a top floor and dormers added. No 59 remains unaltered.

82/84 Montacute Road (26D), to the west, an Italianate pair, probably c1860, with to the left a full-height gently bowed extension, probably of the late 1860s.

27. St Dunstans College, a splendid large Gothic building of 1888, multi-gabled with a grand central entrance, three oriels, and lots of terracotta decoration. To the right is the dining-hall of 1961, largely glazed, suspended on pillars, with a dramatic roof which swoops up to form rounded loops at each end.

28. *Stanstead Grove. It is amazing to find this rural survival, a private close, off the South Circular Road. At the end nos 1/3 are c1855, and to the right nos 4/8 are probably of the 1860s. In front of nos 1/3, The Coach House, with its steep gabled front, was the coach-house for Stanstead Villa, a large mid 19th century house to the west of Stanstead Grove, demolished in the late 19th century.

29. Blythe Hill Tavern, 319 Stanstead Road, a pleasing pub c1866, rounding the corner of Blythe Hill Lane.

30. Blythe Hill Lane is a rural lane leading from Stanstead Road up to Blythe Hill Fields. Together with neighbouring roads - Winterstoke Road, Blythe Hill, Ravensbourne Road - it forms a distinct enclave, with many houses of the 1860s, within an otherwise predominantly Edwardian area.

Note on 2 Blythe Hill Lane, a late 19th century house, two recent sundials designed by Ray Ashley - one on the chimneystack with the legend 'Time can do much', and one on the west side with the legend 'The day flies on'.

31. Blythe Hill Fields has in the centre a large grassed mound, 70 metres high, which provides sensational *views on all sides except to the west; there is a particularly good panorama to the north, covering Shooters Hill, Hilly Fields with Prendergast School, Canary Wharf, and the National Westminster Tower. Blythe Hill House, built 1842, demolished c1895, was to the south on Blythe Hill Lane, and its grounds became a large part of the Fields.

32. Stanstead Lodge, 260 Stanstead Road. A large and fanciful stuccoed villa, probably of 1842, with battlemented front and west side, and Tudor features.

33. St Georges Church, Vancouver Road, the parish church of Perry Hill. It is a large and imposing Gothic ragstone church of 1880 by William Coppard Banks, with many individual features; however, it is now disused and inaccessible. The large square pinnacled tower was heightened in 1887. The west front is unusual, with twin gabled porches flanking an apsidal baptistery, and a rose window (now boarded up) above. Most windows have fanciful tracery consisting of foiled circles.

> There is absolutely no admission to the church interior, as the building is considered unsafe. It is likely that it will be demolished, in which case the famous stained glass (in the rose window) by Henry Holiday of 1900 will be preserved and used elsewhere.

The **Vicarage** to the west, 1 Vancouver Road, is a substantial and handsome purple brick mansion of 1885 with a good Gothic window.

In Carholme Road is **St Georges Church Hall**, originally St Georges Sunday School and Parish Room of 1889, now serving as the Church; it is basically Gothic and, like the church, has some distinctive features.

34. 37 Woolstone Road has a plaque which is a copy of a GLC blue plaque in North End Road, Hampstead, as follows: 'John Linnell 1792-1882 painter lived here, William Blake 1757-1827 poet and artist stayed here as his guest'. Neither Linnell nor Blake lived in or had any known connection with Perry Hill, and this house was built after their deaths, probably in the late 1880s.

Opposite, **18 Woolstone Road**, of 1891, has some remarkable pargetting on an upper floor and in a gable.

35. 145 Perry Hill is a fine late 19th century house, with a rustic porch and a substantial projecting polygonal bay. It was formerly the home of the omnibus entrepreneur Thomas Tilling *(see Catford 52)*.

Behind, **no 143** is a surviving outbuilding of Perry Hill Farm, probably early 19th century.

36. Rutland Arms, 55 Perry Hill, a pleasing and harmonious pub c1866. Behind, nos 1/25 Rutland Walk form a long terrace, of the 1860s.

In **Rutland Park**, a short distance to the south, are two striking terraced groups, probably of the 1860s. Nos 2/8 all have projecting battlemented bay windows, nos 4/6 share a shaped gable. Nos 10/16 are a unified composition, the end houses with short square towers.

37. The Elms, Elm Lane. An old farm-house of the 1790s, with bays c1863 and a porch which is a modern replica of the original.

38. Rathfern School, a pleasant London School Board building of 1887, distinguished by tall pedimented windows which protrude into the gables; the smaller building to the south is of 1900.

39. The former Catford Police Station, 128 Catford Hill, an impressive long red brick building of 1891.

Just to the north, **King's Church**, or Catford Hill Baptist Church, built 1880; under the gabled east end are chequerwork and a Gothic window.

40. Vineyard Close. A sequence of staggered terraces of 1972, part brick part weatherboarded, form a pleasing and intriguing pattern along a winding road.

Just to the north, a gate from Catford Hill gives access to a footpath, which leads down across a green to the River Ravensbourne and then continues through a lightly wooded area until after a short distance you can see the **confluence of the Ravensbourne and Pool Rivers (40A)**. The Ravensbourne, which is here narrower than the Pool, sweeps away to the left and cannot be followed on foot. A footbridge takes you to the east bank of the Pool, and a path continues to a bridge at Broadmead (where the remains of a Roman road, the Lewes Way, were found 1969), and then to the Pool River Walk at Bell Green *(see Sydenham 13)*. The Mid Kent Line runs to the east of the River Pool; just to the north of the confluence it is crossed on a skewed bridge by the Catford Loop Line.

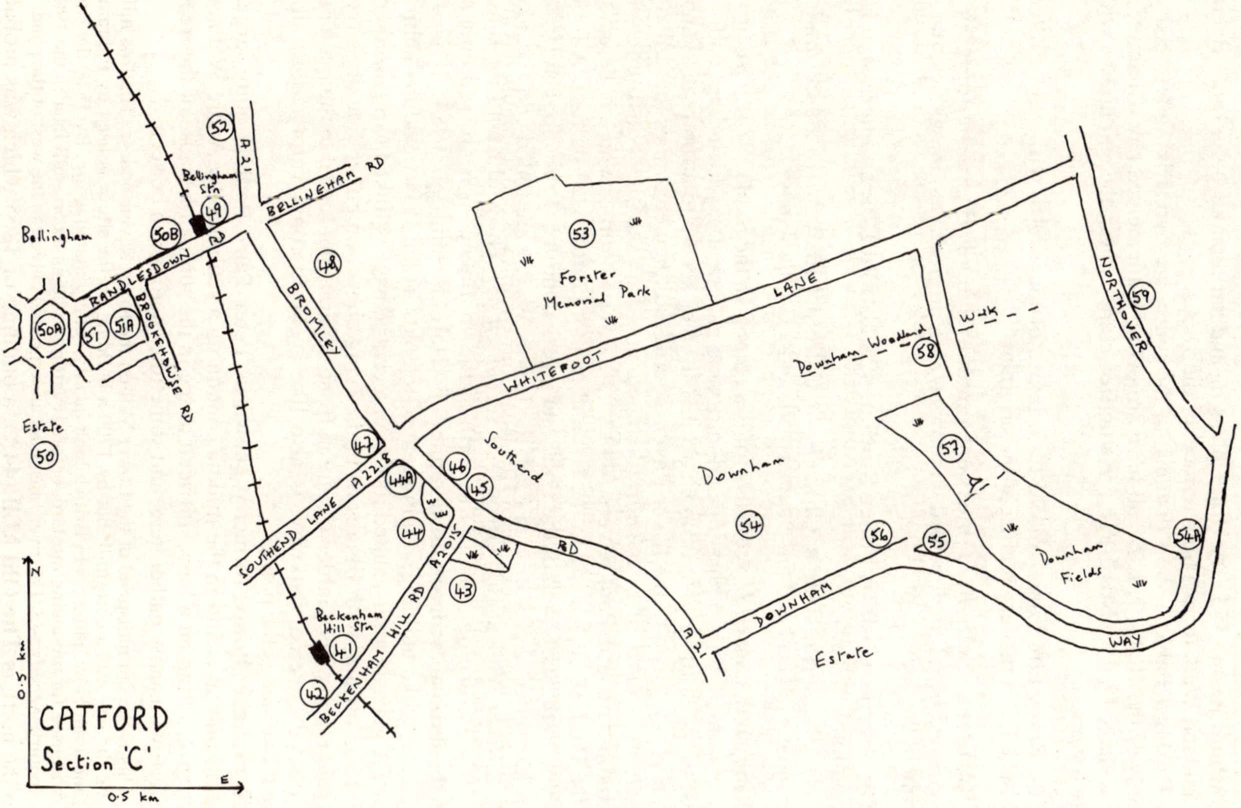

CATFORD
Section 'C'
0·5 km
0·5 km
N
E
Bellingham
Bellingham Stn
Beckenham Hill Stn
Estate
RANDLESDOWN RD
BROOKEHOWSE RD
BELLINGHAM RD
A21
BROMLEY
WHITEFOOT LANE
SOUTHEND LANE A2218
BECKENHAM HILL RD A2015
Southend RD
Forster Memorial Park
Downham
Downham Woodland Walk
NORTHOVER
DOWNHAM WAY
Downham Fields
Estate
41
42
43
44
44A
45
46
47
48
49
50
50A
50B
51
51A
52
53
54
54A
55
56
57
58
59

CATFORD

Gazetteer

Section 'C' SOUTHEND, BELLINGHAM & DOWNHAM

41. Beckenham Hill Station, on the Catford Loop Line, retains its original red brick gabled building of 1892 on the 'up' side.

42. *The Annunciation and St Augustine Church, a striking circular Roman Catholic church of 1964 designed by Raglan Squires. It is of red brick, with the entrance between fortress-like circular drums, and is lit by zig-zag clerestory windows and a central lantern with copper fins. Inside *(call at the adjoining Presbytery or phone 0181-695 1092)*, it is a church 'in the round'.

43. The Meadows Estate. An estate of 1990 with wavy brick terraces pleasingly laid out along curving roads. It replaced the Flower House Estate of c1950, which was built in more traditional style; however, five older blocks have been retained and incorporated in the new estate. To the east there are greens on either side of the River Ravensbourne, whose banks retain a natural appearance here.

> Just south of here on the river was the Upper Mill, which was a corn mill, and a large mill-pond. The mill ceased operation in the 1880s. *See also 44.*

At the junction of Beckenham Hill Road and Bromley Road, is an obelisk fountain of 1897 commemorating the diamond jubilee of Queen Victoria.

44. *Homebase Store was designed by Harold Hamilton 1984. It is a great conservatory-like building, reminiscent of the old Crystal Palace and the Palm House at Kew. A glazed barrel-vaulted roof over a central nave is linked to a glazed entrance hall like an atrium, with figures of birds flying above; on either side are silver-grey steel clad ranges. The Garden Centre in front, separate but linked to the main building by a glazed covered walkway, is also like a glazed conservatory, quite dramatic where it overhangs the pond.

***Homebase Pond**, formerly known as Peter Pan's Pool, is quite large, with fountains and an island in the middle containing a sculpture by André Wallace 1984 of two girls sitting on a fence, difficult to see in the summer because of the trees. Lots of waterfowl usually gather here, and sometimes herons can be seen.

> This is the old mill-pond of the Lower Mill on the River Ravensbourne. The first mill on the site was a corn-mill, but by 1709 a building on the site was used by Ephraim and John How, pioneers in British high quality cutlery manufacture. By 1810 the site was used for producing mustard, before reverting to being a corn-mill later in the 19th century. *See also 43.* The river runs in an underground culvert to the west of the pond.

To the north is **The Old Mill (44A)**, a building of 1865 which was probably the engine house of the 19th century corn-mill. Now an architectural salvage yard.

45. The Green Man, 355 Bromley Road, a very large pub, rebuilt c1935, part neo-Georgian and part mock-Tudor.
>There was a pub on the site in the 18th century, in a small cottage. It became a popular resort after the tramway arrived in 1914.

46. *Church of St John the Baptist. The entrance from Bromley Road leads through an iron arch with Art Nouveau detail into the grounds of a fascinating complex.

Ahead is the Church, of 1928 by Sir Charles Nicholson. The church is of brick, with some Gothic features, particularly in the transepts. The chancel has three bays. Only two bays of the nave were built - if completed, it would have been of cathedral-like proportions, extending almost to the main road; the unused space has been used for a seating area on a lawn.

The *interior is of great interest *(call at the Rectory)*. Its enormous dimensions and the ample light make it very impressive. There is no chancel arch, the nave being continuous with the raised chancel, and there are high stone arches to the transepts. There are massive round arcade piers in both chancel and nave, and a Tudor style wooden roof with about 150 gilt bosses (each one different). The altar is in the crossing, with a fine corona above by John Hayward 1977.

The north aisle is a Forster memorial chapel *(see below)*, with wall monuments to John Forster 1834 and Elizabeth Forster 1837 by Robert Sievier, and to Harriet Forster 1839, all brought from the old chapel, as well as other more recent wall tablets to members of the family; in the aisle is a memorial with a recumbent effigy in military uniform by Cecil Thomas commemorating John and Alfred Forster who died in the 1914-18 War. The Forster family hatchment is at the west end of the nave.

To the south is the *old chapel, now the church hall. It was built as a chapel-of-ease for the Forster family in 1824. It is simple and attractive, with a Tuscan porch, cupola and round-headed windows. The interior has been completely remodelled.

Behind is the *Rectory, a stuccoed rural vernacular building, designed by Sir Charles Nicholson 1921 in a style completely different from anything else around. It is quite large, built for the chapel but in the knowledge that the main church was to be built.
>The Forster family had resided at The Hall, Southend, which was located where Whitefoot Lane joins Bromley Road, since the 18th century. From c1800 John Forster started acquiring property to make them amongst the largest landowners in the Lewisham area. The old chapel had been their proprietory chapel. The most eminent member of the family was Henry William Forster (1866-1936), later Lord Forster, MP for Bromley 1892-1919. The family left the area c1914, though Lord Forster donated the land on which the new church and rectory were built, and also the land for the Forster Memorial Park *(see 53)*. The Hall was demolished in 1937.

47. The Tiger's Head, 350 Bromley Road, an imposing modern pub c1949, refurbished in 1974; it is set back from the main road behind two small greens.
>The How family *(see 44)* occupied a house on the site, but there has been a pub here since 1744.

48. Passfields, an estate built for Lewisham Council by Maxwell Fry and Jane Drew 1950. A gently curved five storey brick range at the back has projecting balconies scattered at intervals; three brick blocks of three storeys pointing towards the road have regular balconies. The estate maintains a crisp appeal. Attractive wooden fencing is a feature, and there are nice greens with trees.

49. Bellingham Station, opened 1892 on the Catford Loop Line, retains its original small red brick booking-hall, and the platforms have their original wooden canopies and iron columns. It was named after Bellingham Farm which was nearby.

50. Bellingham Estate was begun in 1920 on former farmland, and largely completed by 1923, though the final section beyond Southend Lane was not completed until 1936. It is a cottage estate (of over 2600 dwellings) with a pleasant village character, a nice semi-formal layout with roads radiating from the central **Bellingham Green (50A)**. The estate is characterised by short and low brick terraces, vernacular with some rustic features, including roofs sweeping down through the upper floor. The Green has mounds, a play area, and a concrete sculpture, Sunstone, by Hamish Horsley 1985. A shopping parade leads to **The Fellowship (50B)**, Randlesdown Road, a mock-Tudor pub of the 1920s.

51. Church of St Dunstan, Bellingham Green, a red brick church of 1925 by Sir Charles Nicholson. The windows are Gothic, the west front has a romanesque-style blind arcade, and to the left is a campanile. It is cut off at the east end, as the chancel and one of the intended four bays of the nave were not built.

The **interior** *(contact the Vicarage at the rear, or phone 0181-698 3291)* seems large and spacious, though the church was not completed. By the entrance door is the font, date unknown; it is said to be early or mid 19th century, and to have been discovered during excavations for the estate. On the west gallery is the Gothic-style organ, which came from the Chapel Royal, St James's Palace, and dates from 1866; it was brought here in 1925 when the Chapel Royal acquired a new one. At the east end of the north aisle is a copy of a painting by Mariotto Albertinelli (1474-1514), 'The Visitation', the original of which is in the Uffizi Gallery, Florence.

Behind, on Brookehowse Road, is **Brookehowse Community Centre (51A)**, a simple red brick building, also by Nicholson, of 1922, which was used as the church before St Dunstans was built.

On the opposite side of Bellingham Green is Christ Church (United Reformed Church), of 1924, small, red brick.

52. Catford Bus Garage, Bromley Road, was opened in 1914 by London General Omnibus Company, and was used by Thomas Tilling 1920-23. The original garage, of red brick with pedimented corner bays, is at the north end, and there is a cream coloured office building of the 1930s, art deco with a rounded corner tower, at the south end.

53. Forster Memorial Park was donated by Lord Forster in 1919 in memory of his sons killed in the war. It consists mainly of a central grassed area surrounded by belts of trees, some of which may be ancient woodland, but overall it is rather featureless.

54. Downham Estate was begun in 1924 on former farmland, and largely completed by 1930, though the section to the north of Whitefoot Lane was not completed until 1939. It is a cottage estate (over 7000 dwellings), with small groups and longer terraces, in traditional brick design, laid out along curving and intersecting roads.

Downham Way winds its way through the estate. Here is the estate's main shopping centre, and also the Downham Tavern. The pub first opened in 1933, and later came to possess the longest unbroken bar in any British pub; it was demolished 1997, and the site was re-opened 1998 to include a Co-op supermarket and a smaller **Downham Tavern (54A)**, both in a vernacular style, interesting and attractive.

55. Church of St Barnabas, Downham Way, a brick building by Sir Charles Nicholson of 1929. The west front has fine brickwork with a large rounded archway, a circular window above, and an asymmetrical bellcote; otherwise the exterior is not dramatic.

The *****interior** *(contact 1 Churchdown, or phone 0181-698 4851)* provides a strong contrast; it is light and spacious, and very powerful, like a Byzantine temple, dominated by four great thick Doric columns of concrete along each side of the nave. You enter first a narthex, which was enclosed in 1981, and there are wonderful perspectives as you walk around, especially from the west gallery. Interesting features include the old organ of 1854, which was originally in The Hall, Southend, was moved in 1922 to the old chapel at St Johns Southend, and was placed here in 1931; the original stone font, wooden pulpit, and painted reredos; a crucifix and two candlesticks of art nouveau design by Sir Charles Nicholson, now in the west gallery.

Alongside is **St Barnabas Hall**, of brick but with dormers, also by Nicholson, of 1926, used as the church before St Barnabas was built.

56. Downham Community Centre, Downham Way, was originally Downham Methodist Church of 1929, and became a community centre c1978; it is of plain brick in harmony with the estate.

57. Downham Fields, a pleasing oblong of grass on a sloping site which undulates and gives good views to the west.

58. Nubia Way, Moorside Road. An interesting close of 13 self-build houses of 1997, based on the Walter Segal concept and supervised by Jon Broome of Architype *(see Forest Hill 2)*. The detached timber-framed houses in a staggered pattern, with upper floors weatherboarded in brown pine, form a very attractive group.

Opposite is **Downham Woodland Walk**, a linear park which runs through part of the estate, with fine mature trees.

59. St Lukes Church, Northover, a simple brick church by Sir Charles Nicholson of 1938, with a bellcote and narthex at the west front, and groups of narrow round-headed windows.

The interior *(call at the vicarage next door, or phone 0181-698 1354)*, is pleasing and spacious; it was rebuilt after war damage, when some unauthentic decorative features were added, like painted ceiling ribs and stained glass windows.

CATFORD

Suggested Walk

It is recommended that the suggested walk be followed in conjunction with the Gazetteer and the maps, and that the Gazetteer be consulted at each location for a detailed description. Many locations described in Sections 'A' and 'B' of the Gazetteer are covered; others have not been included, as they would add too much to the length of the walk. The walk begins and ends at Catford Bridge or Catford Stations, which are very close to each other. Distance approx 4 kilometres.
Try to make an advance arrangement - see the gazetteer - to view the interior of St Laurence Church.

On leaving **Catford Bridge Station (1)** or **Catford Station (2)**, turn left eastwards along Catford Road, then left along Doggett Road until you reach Holbeach Road. Note **Holbeach School (5)** and its **lodge**; a nearby bridge over the railway gives a view of **Catford Greyhound Stadium (3A)**. Walk along Holbeach Road to Rushey Green, passing **Holbeach Baptist Church (6)**. Turn right, note the great cat outside **The Catford Centre (13)**, then cross the road; looking back, note on the corner of Holbeach Road the upper storeys of **120/4 Rushey Green (7)**.

You are now outside **Eros House (14)**. Proceed southwards on the east side of the road, passing **The Black Horse and Harrow (15)** and the **ABC cinema (18)**, until you reach **St Laurence Church (19)** - try to see the interior. Continue along Bromley Road to **Priory House School (20)**, with the **Forster Estate (21)** to your left, then cross the road and return along the west side.

Passing **Laurence House (24A)**, you come to the oval-shaped building comprising **Lewisham Theatre (23)** and **Lewisham Town Hall (24)**. Bear left past the Town Hall to **Catford Broadway (25)**; detour along Thomas Lane to see **Elmwood (25)**.

Passing the two Stations, turn right into **Ravensbourne Park**, noting **nos 7, 11/15** and **25/27 (26A)** on the left. Continue until you come to **nos 60/62 (26B)** on the right, then cross Ravensbourne Park Gardens to **57/59 Ravensbourne Park Crescent (26C)**. Bear left down Polsted Road, and you emerge opposite **82/84 Montacute Road (26D)**. Turn right, continue and take the footpath left into **Blythe Hill Fields (31)** for the **views**. Take the footpath to the left down into **Blythe Hill Lane (30)**, noting **Blythe Hill Tavern (29)** at the bottom, then turn left along Stanstead Road. Take a look at **Stanstead Grove (28)** to the left.

Continue past **St Dunstans College (27)** into Catford Road, and you are soon back at the two Stations. If you have time, on reaching Catford Road, turn right along Catford Hill and you quickly come to a gate on the left which leads to the **confluence of the Ravensbourne and Pool Rivers (40A)**; retrace steps and continue to the two Stations.

HITHER GREEN

Introduction

There was a medieval hamlet called Romborough which probably included most of the northern part of Hither Green. Recent research by Godfrey Smith suggests that, like Kidbrooke a few kilometres away to the east, it disappeared because of the Black Death in the 14th century.

The growth of housing

The earliest subsequent evidence of any buildings at all in Hither Green comes in the mid 18th century. A number of larger houses were built in the early 19th century; of these, the only survivor is the rear part of St Swithuns Vicarage, dating from c1823. The actual green, which was located all around the road junction by the entrance to Hither Green Hospital, was enclosed by 1819. Development between the 1840s and the 1870s included the mansion of Mountsfield and villas in The Woodlands (none of these survive), and houses in Beacon Road and adjacent parts of Hither Green Lane (a few of these survive).

Hither Green is now densely developed, mostly during the Edwardian period after the opening of Hither Green Station in 1895. By far the largest development was the St Germans Estate, a large estate, developed by Cameron Corbett and built between 1896 and 1913; apart from Hither Green Cemetery, the estate occupies the whole of the southern part of the area, as well as a smaller part to the north of Brownhill Road, leading up to Hither Green Station.

Churches

The growth of housing led to the building of some remarkable churches. The two Anglican churches remain - St Swithuns, the only surviving complete church by the eminent architect Ernest Newton, in Gothic style, unusual for Newton, whose early Queen Anne style is best exemplified in the adjacent Vicarage; and St Andrews, by Philip Robson (son of the London School Board architect Edward Robson) with its powerful interior. Most of the original nonconformist churches have gone, an exception being the fanciful Brownhill Road Baptist Church. The Roman Catholic church, the Holy Cross, is outside the area, and is included under Catford.

Hither Green Hospital

Hither Green Hospital, with its dominant water tower, is the focal point of the northern part of the area. It was built in 1896, and has some splendid buildings in a fine environment. It closed in 1997, and the future use of the site is the subject of considerable local controversy.

HITHER GREEN

Gazetteer

(See map on page 82)

1. Hither Green Station did not open until 1895, though Hither Green Rail Junction had been formed 30 years earlier at the junction of the Tonbridge Line, opened 1865, and the Dartford Loop Line, opened 1866. No station building on the street now remains, the main access since 1974 being up a ramp from a tunnel (note on the tunnel wall 'Meridian Line Longitude Zero') to the booking hall located between the Tonbridge and the Dartford Loop platforms; the platforms for each line are linked by separate covered iron bridges.

The original station building of 1895 was in Staplehurst Road, it closed in 1974. Another station building was opened in Springbank Road for the St Germans Estate *(see 19)* in 1896; this closed in 1968, the red brick gateposts remaining, and the site is now used by a timber merchant. However, to the left the original **stationmaster's house (1A)** of 1896, 69 Springbank Road, survives.

To the south, between Hither Green Station and Grove Park Station, are the Hither Green sidings and marshalling yard, opened from 1899. This vast complex is best seen from the footbridge by Hither Green Nature Reserve *(see Grove Park 4)*.

2. The Station, 14 Staplehurst Road, a fanciful pub of 1906 with the inscription 'Station Hotel', at the centre of a small Edwardian shopping centre.

3. Ennersdale School, Leahurst Road, has a great central building of 1897 with urns on top and flanked by dramatic corner towers; to the south is an end pavilion of 1902 with a linking section also of 1902, and to the north a postwar end pavilion with a linking section of 1908.

4. Queens Arms, 63 Courthill Road, a classical pub c1866, with a portrait of Queen Victoria on the front and the inscription 'Queens Arms Hotel & Tavern'.

5. Sir John Morden, 62 Campshill Road, an Italianate pub c1869, with a portrait of Morden, founder of Morden College, Blackheath, to whom the land belonged.

6. An obelisk of 1721 is an astonishing survival in Monument Gardens, a development of imaginatively grouped vernacular houses in closes, of 1990. This was formerly the grounds of Campshill House (built 1824 on Hither Green Lane, demolished 1947), and the obelisk was probably imported as an ornamental feature.

7. The Spotted Cow, 104 Hither Green Lane, an attractive classical pub, c1867, heavily rusticated.

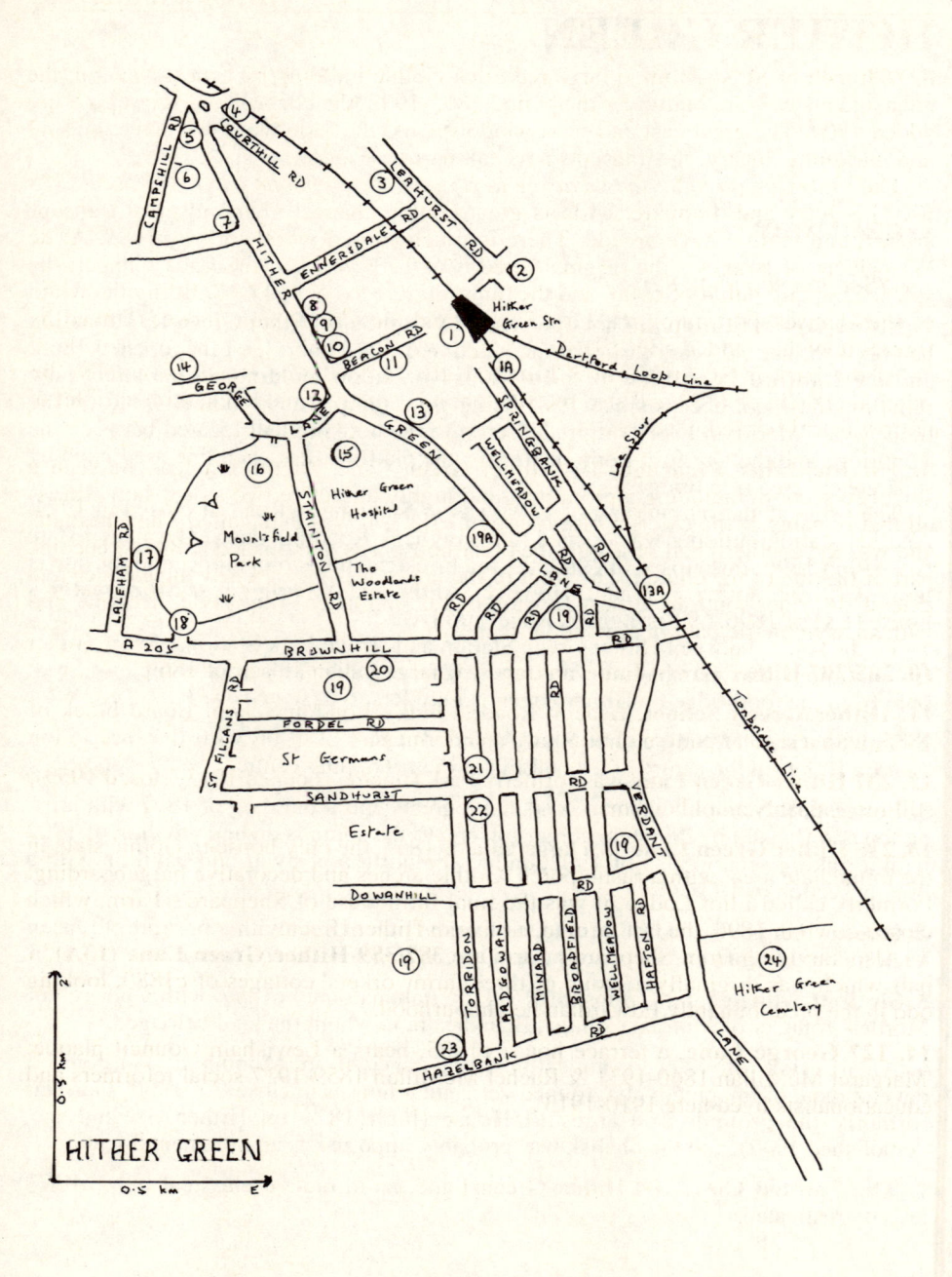

HITHER GREEN

8. *Church of St Swithun, a large red brick Gothic building by Ernest Newton; the nave and aisles were built over the period 1892-1902, the chancel and transepts were added 1904. The great east and west windows, and the aisle windows, have unusual and intriguing tracery; the transepts have tall narrow windows.

The *interior *(contact the vicarage next door, or telephone 0181-852 5088, 318 7531)* is lofty and dramatic, with its great Gothic chancel arch and great transept arches, and Gothic nave arcade. There is much carved woodwork by H. & A. de Wispelaere of Bruges - the original reredos of 1906, now in the Lady Chapel; the splendid square pulpit of 1906; and the fantastic reredos of 1911-18, filling the width of the chancel, portraying the Last Supper and the Crucifixion above, flanked by figures in niches (added after 1918).

At the back is **St Swithuns Church Hall**, St Swithuns Road, originally the mission church, of 1884 and also by Newton; it is small, of red brick, with a triplet of narrow round-headed windows.

9. *St Swithuns Vicarage, 191 Hither Green Lane. At the rear can be seen a stuccoed section, including a prominent and highly attractive two storey bow; this is all that remains of the exterior of a house of c1823. It was then called The Chesnuts, and was the southern half of a pair; the other house was demolished c1891 to become part of the site of the church. The front of the house was given a new appearance and extended further south by Ernest Newton c1892, in Queen Anne style, irregular and with an asymmetric pattern of window shapes.

10. 205/207 Hither Green Lane, an imposing large Italianate pair of 1869.

11. Hither Green School, Beacon Road, a bulky London School Board block of 1885, with a regular pattern of windows and dormers.

12. 232 Hither Green Lane was formerly Park Cinema (opened 1913, closed 1959), still recognisably an old cinema.

13. 295 Hither Green Lane is a large villa of 1867, the only house in Gothic style in the immediate area, with a rustic porch, Gothic arches and decorative bargeboarding. Formerly called Eliot Lodge, it was the final farmhouse of Sheppard's Farm, which closed down in 1896, the last farm to survive in Hither Green.

Also surviving from Sheppard's Farm are **387/389 Hither Green Lane (13A)**, a pair which was originally a group of three farmworkers' cottages of c1880, looking odd in the predominantly Edwardian neighbourhood.

14. 127 George Lane, a terrace house c1905, bears a Lewisham Council plaque: 'Margaret McMillan 1860-1931 & Rachel McMillan 1859-1917 social reformers and educationalists lived here 1910-1913'.

15. *Hither Green Hospital, originally a fever hospital known as Park Hospital, was designed by Edwin Hall 1896; it closed summer 1997, and there is at present no access to the main part of the site, the future of which is the subject of considerable local controversy. A small and uninspired housing estate, Mountsfield Gardens, occupies a small part of the site.

Interesting original features include: the former waiting-rooms, a curved building with Dutch gables and colonnades with fluted terracotta columns; turret-fronted wards, connected by splendid brick covered walkways; a tall and powerful brick water cum clock tower over 30 metres high, with a gallery; and an octagonal boiler chimney, which has lost its top cupola. These impressive buildings remain at present within a pleasing rural environment with fine trees.

16. Mountsfield Park opened as a public park in 1905, occupying the grounds of the mansion Mountsfield, and was extended to its present size in stages up to 1933.

> Mountsfield was built 1845, demolished 1905; no trace of the mansion or its outbuildings now remains. Among the fields subsequently absorbed into the Park was the ground used by Charlton Athletic Football Club 1921-24.

Mainly open parkland, it descends steeply southwards, providing spectacular *views towards the west; clearly visible are Hilly Fields, Oak of Honor Hill, Honor Oak Road and Sydenham Hill. The cupola of The Dartmouth pub *(see 17)* is conspicuous from here.

17. The Dartmouth, 77 Laleham Road, an incredible fantasy pub c1900, with a wonderful corner cupola topped by a weathervane, recessed balconies at first floor level, projecting rounded bays on the ground floor, and lots of extravagant ornamental flourishes.

18. Redfern Road, a close backing onto Mountsfield Park, by Royston Summers 1981. Six pairs of three storey houses are linked by glazed staircases. Each house has a fully glazed inner bay and a largely brick outer bay. This was an early example of partial solar heating with roof panels.

19. *St Germans Estate. A large estate, developed by Cameron Corbett and built between 1896 and 1913. The estate lies mostly to the south of Brownhill Road, between Verdant Lane and St Fillans Road, but there is a smaller part to the north of Brownhill Road, leading up to Hither Green Station.

> Cameron Corbett, later Lord Rowallan, was a major Edwardian developer in the London area. There are no pubs or off-licences on his estates. Besides Hither Green, his other major estates are at Eltham Park, Ilford and Forest Gate.

The houses are of red brick, with stone dressings; they are well-designed and solidly built, and are mostly in long terraces, which can become monotonous. But there is variety in size and detailing, and the overall effect is often very attractive. There is some later infill, but not much. Note in particular:

(i) St Fillans Road, of 1898, particularly attractive, with terraces in warm red brick and minimal stone dressings, the west side being very harmonious.

(ii) Fordel Road, of 1900, has a particularly fine sequence of houses with alternating female and bearded and/or moustachioed male mask keystones over the entrance archways. Alternating female and male masks occur in many other roads, with good examples in Ardgowan Road, of 1898, and Hafton Road, of 1902.

(iii) **Brownhill Road**, of 1898, between Verdant Lane and the Baptist Church, has stately terraces of double-fronted houses, some with masks and many with festoons.

(iv) **Wellmeadow Road**, of 1899, has some impressive terraces with fine stone dressings and dentilled pediments. There are similar groups in the part of Torridon Road, of 1898, to the north of Brownhill Road.

(v) The southern part of **Hither Green Lane**, of 1896, has a number of attractive double-fronted houses. To the north, just outside the estate, **nos 246/274 (19A)**, formerly known as Central Market, are three storey shops c1905 with stone framed windows along the upper floors, and ball finials on the roof between each shop.

20. Brownhill Road Baptist Church, an interesting and fanciful terraced group, comprising the church of 1903, with swirling Gothic tracery in the windows, a small tower with spire and pinnacles, and the church hall of 1937.

21. Torridon Library. A low baroque building of 1907, with lots of classical motifs in red brick and Doultons grey terracotta, including Ionic columns flanking the entrance, and a striking concave-faceted octagonal turret. The interior, lit by a great glazed dome, is also of interest, with classical detail in the plasterwork.

22. Church of St Andrew, Torridon Road. A large red brick Gothic church of 1904 by Philip Robson. Great east and west windows with gargoyles, and tall narrow windows along the aisles. The chancel has flying buttresses with gargoyles.

The ***interior** is powerful, more magnificent than can be imagined outside, dominated by the arcades and by the glory of the east window.

The church is normally open Wednesday mornings 1000-1200, otherwise contact the Vicarage, 135 Wellmeadow Road, 0181-697 2600.

Wide nave and narrow aisles, with arcades of tall narrow Gothic arches in red brick which extend into the chancel. The chancel has a raised marble sanctuary, very intricate ironwork and finely carved woodwork in art nouveau style. The brilliant stained glass in the east window is a war memorial of 1921 by Martin Travers, who was also responsible for the flanking narrow windows, the windows in the Lady Chapel (except the eastern one), and the windows around the chancel (except the easternmost one on the north side, to Henry Purcell, by Peter Cormack 1998 but based loosely on a design by Travers). The west window and the windows in the nave have no stained glass, but are partly coloured with nice intricate patterns.

At the rear is the original mission church of 1900, now the church hall.

23. Torridon School is formed by a group of quite elegant low buildings, with flowing Dutch gables, built for the London County Council 1906.

24. Hither Green Cemetery, opened 1873 as Lee Cemetery. An irregular and romantic cemetery with winding lanes, crowded with tombstones. Two elaborate Gothic ragstone chapels by Francis Thorne survive, one with a belfry and the other with a spire, both with gargoyles. Near the further chapel is a fine Gothic mausoleum 1903 to John Taylor and family. Just to the right after entering, behind a hedge, is a headstone of 1998, promoted by the Lewisham Local History Society, to Leland Duncan (1862-1923), the Lewisham local historian.

To the south and providing a vivid contrast is **Lewisham Crematorium**, of 1956, set in fine though rather formal landscaping with a pond.

GROVE PARK

Introduction

Grove Park is a small area to the east of the railway line to Tonbridge; it retains the atmosphere of a late Victorian railway suburb. Though most of the older houses have been destroyed, the extent of the Victorian community is still distinguishable by the street plantings of large trees, first set down c1891.

The coming of the railway

The railway to Sevenoaks and Tonbridge was laid down across an area of farmland (part of the old parish of Lee) in 1866, but Grove Park Station did not open until 1871. A new line from Grove Park to Bromley North was opened in 1878.

Housing in the area to the east of the railway line began to develop, initially quite slowly - by 1879 there were just a few large houses in Baring Road and Chinbrook Road. In the 1880s many more houses were added in these and neighbouring streets. The first stage of St Augustines Church was built in 1886. In 1899 the foundation stone was laid of one of the last workhouses to be built in the country.

At the same time Lee was growing southwards towards the area along Baring Road and Burnt Ash Hill.

The spread of housing

It was not until the interwar years that the expansion of housing covered the area. The Metropolitan Borough of Lewisham built the Grove Park Estate between Chinbrook Meadows and Marvels Lane 1926-9. The area to the west of the railway line became covered by the vast Downham Estate *(see Catford 54)*, built by the London County Council 1924-30. Private developers filled in the gaps to the east of Baring Road and in the area going towards Lee; these developments, mostly of the 1930s, included the distinctive chalet-style houses in and around Exford Road and Pragnell Road.

Postwar

Most of the remaining older and larger houses made way for more intensive housing developments after 1945, and not many of the large late Victorian houses have survived - a few in Chinbrook Road, a pair in Luffman Road, a solitary large house in Somertrees Avenue, and groups in Amblecote Road. In the early 1990s a housing estate replaced most of the workhouse buildings which since 1926 had been Grove Park Hospital, though the fine buildings fronting Marvels Lane by Thomas Dinwiddy have been retained.

GROVE PARK

Gazetteer

(See map on page 88)

1. Grove Park Station. An interesting railway station, opened 1871 on the Tonbridge line, which had been laid down through the area in 1866. The present building on Baring Road results from rebuilding in 1905, though a fragment of the original weatherboarded building survives to the left. From the station building an amazing network of long covered walkways leads down to the five platforms, which have long canopies and are linked by a rather picturesque bridge. The right-hand platform serves the branch to Bromley North, opened 1878.

2. The Baring Hall Hotel, opposite the station. A fine pub c1882 in Queen Anne style by Ernest Newton, with some individual features. Note the dormer windows, the projecting bay linked to an attic storey, and the first floor balcony. At the rear the former coach-house and stables of 1892 can be distinguished.

Opposite, **372 Baring Road** is the sole survivor of a group of four shops of the early 1880s.

3. St Augustines Church, Baring Road. A squat Gothic ragstone church, looking truncated and unappealing, as the west end was clearly put on an unfinished church and the east end is a temporary structure following removal of the apse c1994 due to subsidence. The chancel of two bays (only the footings of the apse remain) and the transepts are of 1886 by Charles Bell. The nave, only partly completed, with three bays instead of five, is of 1912 by Percy Leeds. The strange brick west front was added in 1967 by Eric Starling, with a low brick narthex in front, part of a group of buildings including the church hall around a courtyard.

However, the ***interior** is worth viewing for its elaborate furnishings, particularly the woodwork and stained glass windows *(contact the vicarage next door at 336 Baring Road, or telephone 0181-857 4941)*. It is lofty and imposing, giving some idea of the scale of the church if it had been completed.

The carved oak woodwork is of 1909-12 by H. & A. de Wispelaere of Bruges, and is quite magnificent - the sumptuously carved and elaborately detailed reredos with canted wings, the delicately carved screens, the choirstalls, the pulpit with its beautiful and eloquently carved figures, and the pyramidal font cover. The font is at the west end of the north aisle, of stone and relatively simple, whereas the font cover (usually on the floor alongside) is elaborately carved.

The Lady Chapel occupies the south transept - the altar is in an arched recess, there is a striking painted reredos by Christopher Webb 1923, and a gothic piscina modelled on a 13th century one in Southwark Cathedral. All the stained glass

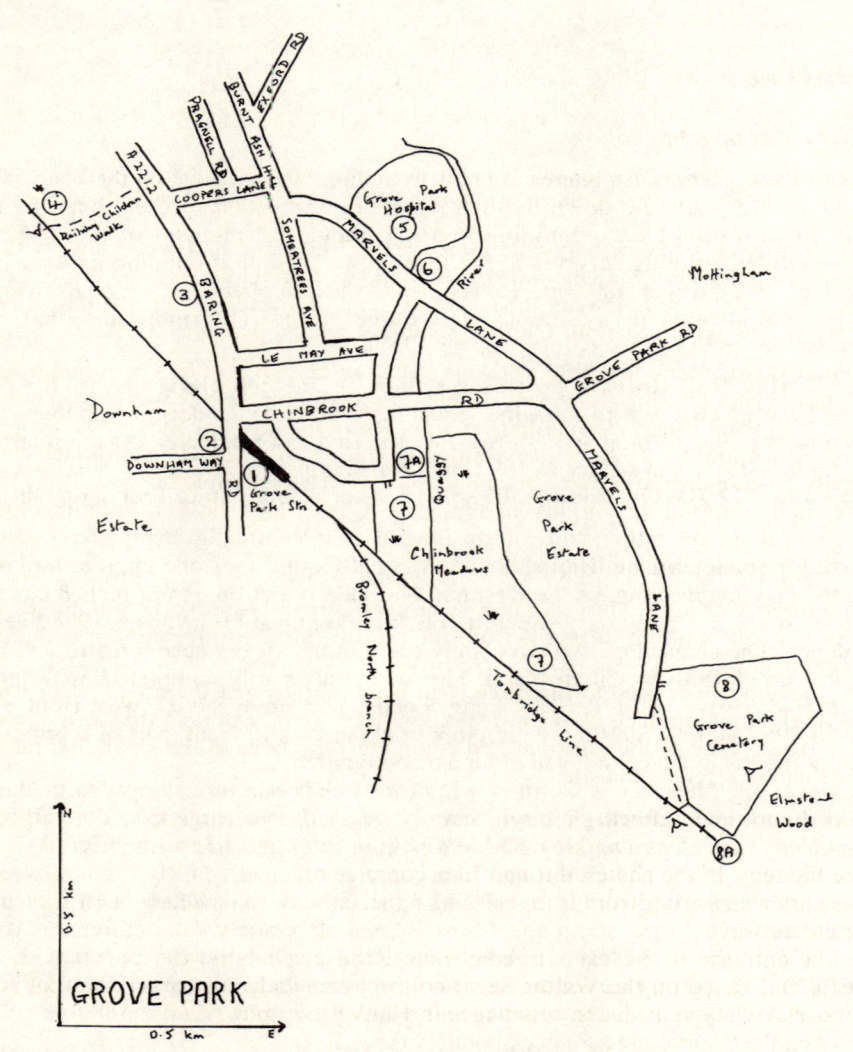

windows in the Lady Chapel are of 1905 by Heaton, Butler & Bayne. The stained glass window just outside in the south aisle is by Dudley Forsyth 1917.

Other windows by Heaton, Butler & Bayne, which were in the apse, have been removed for future re-use.

The west wall has a great crucifix made in 1919 for St Marks Church Plumstead (now demolished), and transferred here 1975; and a vivid stained glass window by the Whitefriars Studios 1966.

4. Hither Green Nature Reserve, accessible from Baring Road by a footpath called Railway Children Walk.

> Edith Nesbit, the children's writer and poet, lived 1894-99 in a house nearby, though her book 'The Railway Children' was written after she had moved to Well Hall, Eltham.

The reserve is an unexpectedly extensive area of grassland and woodland, with a stream and a pond, alongside the railway line. The footpath continues to a bridge over the railway, giving good views of the railway sidings and yards between Hither Green Station and Grove Park Station, and then continues into the Downham Estate.

5. Former Grove Park Hospital, Marvels Lane. An extensive complex of buildings, which has been a housing estate since 1994. Originally on the site was a workhouse for the Greenwich Board of Guardians designed by Thomas Dinwiddy 1899-1902; it became a hospital in 1926 and a residential home in 1977. The grounds were originally much more extensive, stretching as far as Mottingham Lane.

The multi-turreted and highly imaginative lodges, and the main admin block which is gabled on either side of its magnificent central archway, have been preserved from the original Dinwiddy buildings.

6. Sydenham Cottages, Marvels Lane. A group of six old farmworkers' cottages of the 1860s, each building different from the others, the only pre-railway buildings surviving in Grove Park.

The Quaggy River used to run directly in front, until it was diverted further east. There is an old pump once used for dealing with the floodwaters in the front garden of no 1. The course of the old river-bed is amongst the trees in the small and rather desolate nature reserve opposite.

7. Chinbrook Meadows. A large, mainly grassed area alongside the railway embankment, opened as a park by the Metropolitan Borough of Lewisham in 1937.

The Quaggy River passes through in a concrete channel (mostly hidden by tall hedges) after emerging from a tunnel under the railway line. Nearby is a footpath under the railway.

By the entrance to the park in Amblecote Road a self-build development of 14 houses (**7A**), based on the Walter Segal concept and under the supervision of Jon Broome of Architype, is due to commence in 1999 *(see Forest Hill 2)*.

8. Grove Park Cemetery, Marvels Lane. A well landscaped cemetery of 1935; to the south is a terrace with an ornamental pool, giving fine views towards Elmstead Wood. Note the contemporary black and white timber Gothic chapel.

Near the entrance to the cemetery, a footpath leads to a footbridge over the railway which provides a good view of the **twin railway tunnels (8A)** under Elmstead Wood, the tunnel to the left of 1865 and the tunnel to the right of 1901.

Notes on some Architects & Artists

(Gazetteer references - S = Sydenham; CP = Crystal Palace; FH = Forest Hill; C = Catford; HG = Hither Green; GP = Grove Park)

Thomas Aldwinckle, 1844-1930 *(FH 22)*. A local architect, he designed Brook Hospital Kidbrooke (the main buildings of which have been preserved), Kentish Town Public Baths, and the Public Baths and Louise House at Forest Hill.

Banks & Barry (Robert Banks, 1813-72, and Charles Barry Jr, 1823-1900), *(S 62)*. Leading architects of the mid Victorian period. Barry, the architect of Dulwich College, was a son of Sir Charles Barry.

Edward Middleton Barry, 1830-80 *(CP 21)*. An architect of many grand buildings, including the Opera House and Floral Hall of 1857 at Covent Garden, and Charing Cross Hotel. He was a son of Sir Charles Barry.

John Francis Bentley, 1839-1902 *(S 30)*. Architect of Westminster Cathedral, in Byzantine style, and of several Roman Catholic churches, in Gothic style.

Bradshaw, Gass and Hope *(C 23)*. Based in Bolton, this firm has been responsible for numerous large buildings in Greater Manchester, most notably the Royal Exchange in Manchester, but also a number of large buildings in the London area.

Isambard Kingdom Brunel, 1806-59 *(CP 3)*. A great Victorian engineer, son of the French-born Sir Marc Brunel. He was responsible for the Great Western Railway (including stations, bridges, tunnels); the Clifton Suspension Bridge; the ships 'Great Britain' (now in Bristol), 'Great Western', and 'Great Eastern' (launched at Millwall, opposite Deptford); and (with his father) the first Thames Tunnel, between Rotherhithe and Wapping.

Ewan Christian, 1814-95 *(FH 40)*. Architectural adviser to the Ecclesiastical Commissioners from 1850. In addition to many churches, he designed the National Portrait Gallery.

Thomas Dinwiddy, 1845-c1926 *(GP 5)*. An architect of South-East London. He designed the Laurie Grove Baths, New Cross; the Roan School for Girls, Greenwich; The Hollies, Sidcup; and Grove Park Hospital.

Maxwell Fry *(C 48)*, leading architect of the modernist style, influenced by Le Corbusier and Gropius. He built a number of notable houses and blocks of flats in the 1930s. Postwar, the partnership of Fry and **Jane Drew** *(C 48)* was responsible for buildings at Chandigarh and Ibadan, and for Pilkingtons Glass Works, St Helens.

Sir Frederick Gibberd *(CP 25)*. A noted modern architect, whose Pullman Court at Streatham was a prewar example of the modernist style. The postwar works of Sir Frederick Gibberd & Partners have been more eclectic - they have included the earlier buildings of Heathrow Airport; early buildings in Harlow New Town; Coutts Bank, Strand; Liverpool Roman Catholic Cathedral; Regents Park Mosque.

Edwin Thomas Hall, 1851-1923 *(HG 15.)*. A leading architect specialising in hospital design. His works included Hither Green Hospital, the Royal Hospital for

Incurables at Norwood, and the Manchester Royal Infirmary; and also Liberty's Store, Regent Street.

Owen Luder *(C 13-14)*. A modern architect, whose practice has built office blocks in a more or less brutalist style, in Bromley, Catford, Hayes (Hillingdon), New Malden, Sidcup and Sutton.

Peter Moro, 1911-98 *(FH 10)*. Leading modern architect, one of the design team for the Royal Festival Hall. Among his more important works were Fairlawn School and his own house, 20 Blackheath Park. He specialised in theatre architecture and design.

Edward Mountford, 1855-1908 *(FH 17)*. An eclectic Edwaridan baroque architect, designer of Sheffield Town Hall, the Old Bailey, Lancaster Town Hall.

Edwin Nash, 1814-84 *(S 18, 25, 47)*. A resident of Sydenham, he specialised in mid Victorian church rebuilds, restorations and extensions, particularly in South East London.

Ernest Newton, 1856-1922 *(HG 8-9; GP 2)*. A pupil of Norman Shaw, and a founder of the Art Workers Guild. He developed the Queen Anne and Arts & Crafts styles into an inventive Neo-Georgian. From the 1890s he designed many houses in Chislehurst and Bickley, and elsewhere.

Sir Charles Nicholson, 1867-1949 *(C 46, 51, 55, 59)*. Architect of numerous churches in a variety of styles throughout the country. Towards the end of his working life he designed four churches in Southend, Downham and Bellingham.

Sir Joseph Paxton, 1803-65 *(S 44, 77B; CP 4)*. When head gardener at Chatsworth he designed the Great Greenhouse there. He went on to lay out Princes Park Liverpool and Birkenhead Park before being selected to build the Crystal Palace. His more traditional buildings include Mentmore Towers.

George Fellowes Prynne, 1853-1927 *(S 8)*. An important architect in the Gothic style, who worked mostly on church building and restoration. He is noted for his chancel screens.

Sir Basil Spence, 1907-76 *(S 74)*. Among his large projects, sometimes in brutalist style, are Knightsbridge Barracks, Thorn House, and Kensington Town Hall.

Charles Harrison Townsend, 1851-1928 *(FH 19, 19A)*. The most brilliant and innovative Arts & Crafts architect in London. His main works were Bishopsgate Institute, Horniman Museum and Whitechapel Art Gallery.

Sir Aston Webb, 1849-1930 *(FH 9)*. Eminent architect in an eclectic Edwardian style. His most famous works were Admiralty Arch, the street front of the Victoria & Albert Museum, and the east front of Buckingham Palace.

William Frederick Woodington, (1806-93) *(CP 8)*. Sculptor of the Coade Stone lion at Westminster Bridge, and of Paxton's bust in Crystal Palace Park.

David Wynne *(CP 16)*. His sculpture can be seen in several outdoor locations in London - St Katherines Dock, Chelsea Embankment, Cadogan Square Gardens, Crystal Palace Park; and also in Ely Cathedral.

Bibliography

including books and publications consulted, and books recommended for further reading, especially for information on local history and architectural detail

London 2: South, by Bridget Cherry & Nikolaus Pevsner (Buildings of England series, Penguin Books, 1983)
The Industrial Archaeology of South East London (Goldsmiths College Industrial Archaeology Group, 1982)
Retracing Canals to Croydon & Camberwell, by Brian Salter (Living History Publications 1986)
Churches in the Hundred of Blackheath, by L. A. J. Baker (Greenwich & Lewisham Antiquarian Society, 1961)
A Walk down the High Street (Lewisham Local Studies Centre)
Charing Cross to Orpington, by Vic Mitchell & Keith Smith (Middleton Press)
London Bridge to East Croydon, by Vic Mitchell & Keith Smith (Middleton Press)
Crystal Palace and Catford Loop, by Vic Mitchell & Keith Smith (Middleton Press)
Looking back at Lewisham (Lewisham Local Studies Centre)
Lewisham History and Guide, by John Coulter (Alan Sutton Publishing, 1994)
Hither Green, 'the Forgotten Hamlet', by Godfrey Smith (1997)
A History of Kings & Princes Garth, by Jad Adams (1993)
Forest Hill and Sydenham, by Adrian Prockter (1987)
The Horniman Sundial Trail (Horniman Trust & British Sundial Society)
Palace of the People, by Graham Reeves (Bromley Libraries, 1986)
The Crystal Palace Park of 1854, by Christine Northeast (1979)
Camille Pissarro at Crystal Palace, by Nicholas Reed (third edition, 1995)
Pissarro up to date in Lewisham, by Ken White
Watering Places in Lewisham, by Ken White (1998)
The Public Houses of Lee & Lewisham, by Ken White (1992)
Grove Park, a History of a Community, by John King (1982)
St Augustines Grove Park 1886-1986, by Kenneth Richardson
A guide to St Augustines Church, Honor Oak (1991)
St Barnabas - the early years 1929-1989, by Jim Greenfield
A History of St Dunstans Church and the Bellingham Estate, by John Colley (1985)
A History of St Laurence Church Catford, by Eleanor Relle (1987)
St Bartholomews Church Sydenham, by Dennis Harrington (1997)
Parish Churches of London, by Basil Clarke (Batsford, 1966)
Catholic Churches of London, by Dennis Evinson (Sheffield Academic Press, 1998)
History of the Borough of Lewisham, by Leland L. Duncan (1908)
Old Ordnance Survey maps, published by Alan Godfrey - Catford 1914; Crystal Palace 1871 & 1894; Dulwich Village 1894 & 1913; Forest Hill 1914; Lower Sydenham 1894; Upper Sydenham 1894 & 1914
Many articles in Journals of the Greenwich Historical Society (formerly Greenwich & Lewisham Antiquarian Society), and of the Lewisham Local History Society

All the above publications, and of course many more books, maps and documents, can be consulted at **Lewisham Local Studies Centre**, Lewisham Library, Lewisham High Street, London SE13 (phone 0181-297 0682).

INDEX

(Gazetteer references - S = Sydenham; CP = Crystal Palace; FH = Forest Hill; C = Catford; HG = Hither Green; GP = Grove Park)

Architects & Artists

G S Agar - FH 49
Thomas Aldwinckle - FH 22
Allies & Morrison - FH 19
Ray Ashley - FH 19, 19A; C 30
William Coppard Banks - C 33
Banks & Barry - S 62
Charles Barry Jr - FH 19A
Edward Barry - CP 21
Stanley Beard - FH 24
Anning Bell - FH 19
Charles Bell - GP 3
John Francis Bentley - S 30
Bradshaw Gass & Hope - C 23
Paul Brookes - FH 27
Jon Broome - FH 2, 35, 44; C 58; GP 7A
Isambard Kingdom Brunel - CP 3
Burlison & Grylls - S 25
Ewan Christian - FH 40
Clayton & Bell - S 25
John Collins - C 19
Sir Ninian Comper - FH 40
Peter Cormack - HG 22
Ralph Covell - C 19
Henry Dawson - S 77B
John de Vaere - FH 19
H. & A. de Wispelaere - HG 8; GP 3
Thomas Dinwiddy - GP 5
Jane Drew - C 48
Hans Feibusch - FH 49
Joseph Fogarty - S 33
Dudley Forsyth - GP 3
Moira Forsyth - S 62
Maxwell Fry - C 48
Sir Frederick Gibberd - CP 25
Goddard & Gibbs - S 8; FH 34
Vincent Grose - FH 4
Charles Gurrey - S 62
Edwin Hall - HG 15
Harold Hamilton - C 44
Val Harding - S 59
Waterhouse Hawkins - CP 16
John Hayward - C 46
Heaton, Butler & Bayne - FH 4; GP 3
Alexander Hennell - S 77D; FH 22
Jonathan Hines - FH 19
Angela Hodgson - FH 19A
Henry Holiday - C 33
Hamish Horsley - C 50
Nathan Jackson - FH 19
C E Kempe - S 62
Herbert Klingst - FH 49

Percy Leeds - GP 3
Rosalyn Loftin - FH 19
Owen Luder - C 13-14
Michael Manser - FH 16
Sydney March - S 16
Donald McMorran - S 51
John Moir - FH 19, 19A
Peter Moro - FH 10
Edward Mountford - FH 17
Edwin Nash - S 18, 25, 47
Ernest Newton - HG 8-9; GP 2
Sir Charles Nicholson - C 46, 51, 55, 59
John Norton - CP 25, 27
David Nye - S 18
William Oakley - FH 4
Georges Palejowski - CP 22
Sir Joseph Paxton - S 44, 77B; CP 4
Sir Edward Poynter - S 62
George Fellowes Prynne - S 8
Raglan Squires - C 42
Elspeth Reid - S 67
Ian Ritchie - CP 12
Philip Robson - HG 22
Gerda Rubinstein - C 24
Edwin Russell - FH 19
Eberhard Schulze - C 24
Sir Giles Gilbert Scott - FH 24, 31A
Walter Segal - S 28B; FH 2, 35; C 58; GP 7
Carter Shapland - C 19
Robert Sievier - C 46
Barry Small - FH 19A
Francis Spear - S 25
Sir Basil Spence - S 74
Eric Starling - GP 3
Royston Summers - HG 18
Steven Sykes - S 67
Symonds Travers Morgan - S 13
Francis Tasker - C 17
Cecil Thomas - C 46
Francis Thorne - HG 24
Harrison Townsend - FH 19, 19A
Martin Travers - HG 22
Hans Unger - C 24
Lewis Vulliamy - S 25
André Wallace - C 44
Walters & Kerr Bate - S 8
Samuel Wanjau - C 19
Sir Aston Webb - FH 9
Christopher Webb - GP 3
Whitefriars Studio - FH 49; GP 3
Henry Wilson - S 25
William Frederick Woodington - CP 8

93

94 - INDEX

Sir Christopher Wren - S 75
David Wynne - CP 16

Churches etc
All Saints - S 6
Annunciation & St Augustine - C 42
Brownhill Road Baptist - HG 20
Christ Church - FH 40
Dietrich Bonhoeffer - FH 49
God of Prophecy - S 17
Grove Centre House - S 77D
Holbeach Baptist - C 6
Holy Cross - C 17
Holy Trinity - S 69
Kingdom Hall - FH 29; C 16
King's Church - C 39
New Church (Swedenborgian) - CP 28
Our Lady & St Philip Neri - S 8
Resurrection - S 67
Sacred Heart Convent - FH 5
St Andrew - HG 22
St Augustines Grove Park - GP 3
St Augustines Honor Oak - FH 4
St Barnabas - C 55
St Bartholomew - S 25
St Dunstan - C 51
St Georges - C 33
St John the Baptist - C 46
St Laurence - C 6, 19, 24A
St Lukes - C 59
St Michaels & All Angels - S 18
St Pauls - FH 17, 27, 29
St Peters - FH 19A
St Philip the Apostle - S 47
St Stephen - S 62
St Swithun - HG 8
Zion Baptist Chapel - FH 33

Housing developments
Bellingham Estate - C 50
Brockley Park Estate - FH 36
Courtside - S 73
Dacres Estate - FH 47
Dawsons Heights - FH 19A
Dorrell Estate - FH 26
Downham Estate - C 54
Forster Estate - C 21
Grove Park Hospital - GP 5
Hillcrest Estate - S 29
Julian Taylor Path - S 77A
Lammas Green - S 51
Lawrie Park Estate - S 34-41
Meadows Estate - C 43
Passfields - C 48
Ravensbourne Park Estate - C 26
New Church Court - CP 28
St Germans Estate - HG 1, 19
St Pauls - FH 28
Self-build - S 28B; FH 2, 35; C 58; GP 7A
Spinney Gardens - CP 22

Sydenham Park Estate - S 69-73
Thackerays Almshouses - C 11
Thorpe Estate - S 21

Industrial archaeology
Boundary markers - S 29, 51, 54, 59, 77A; CP 14; FH 3
Catford Bus Garage - C 52
Crystal Palace Museum - CP 2
Honor Oak Pumping Station -FH 8
Horniman Conservatory - FH 19
Old Mill - C 44
Pillar boxes - FH 31
Railway bridges - CP 26, 27; C 3
Railway stations - S 1, 3, 12, 29, 61; CP 1, 21, 26; FH 1, 20; C 1, 2, 41, 49; HG 1; GP 1
Railway track-beds - S 29, 56; CP 21; FH 7, 19A
Railway tunnels - S 29, 56; CP 1, 21; GP 8A
Reservoirs - CP 5, 11, 15; FH 8A, 12
Shops & stores - S 14, 22, 24, 77C; C 13, 16, 44, 54; HG 19A
Sundials - FH 19, 19A; C 30
Sydenham Gas Works - S 15, 16
Telephone kiosks - FH 24, 31A
Water towers - CP 3; HG 15

Leisure
ABC Cinema - C 18
Capitol Cinema - FH 24
Catford Greyhound Stadium - C 3
Childrens zoo - CP 17
Concert platform - CP 12
Crofton Leisure Centre - C 4
Crystal Palace Museum - CP 2
CUE - FH 19
Downham Community Centre - C 56
Horniman Museum - FH 19
Lewisham Theatre - C 23
Livesey Memorial Hall - S 16
National Sports Centre - CP 9
Park Cinema - HG 12

Parks & open spaces
Baxter Field - S 76
Bellingham Green - C 50
Blythe Hill Fields - C 31
Brenchley Gardens - FH 7
Chinbrook Meadows - GP 7
Crystal Palace Park - CP 1-20
Dacres Wood Nature Reserve - FH 48
Downham Fields - C 57
Downham Woodland Walk - C 58
Dulwich Upper Wood - CP 23
Forster Memorial Park - C 53
Grove Park Cemetery - GP 8
Hither Gren Cemetery - HG 24
Hither Green Nature Reserve - GP 4
Honor Oak Cemetery - FH 9
Horniman Gardens - FH 19A

INDEX - 95

Ladywell Fields - C 3
Mayow Park - S 20
Mountsfield Park - HG 16
Oak of Honor Hill - FH 3
Ravensbourne Park Gardens - C 26
River walks - S 13; C 3, 40, 43
Sydenham Hill Wood - S 55-56
Sydenham Wells Park - S 45

People
Edward Aveling - S 27
John Logie Baird - S 59
George Baxter - S 76; FH 40
Mary Baxter - S 69, 76; FH 40
Charles Bayer - FH 12
George Bell - FH 49
Charles Ash Body - S 49
Dietrich Bonhoeffer - FH 17, 49
Walter Cobb - S 24
Jim Connell - FH 39
Cameron Corbett - HG 19
Arthur Dorrell - FH 25-26
Leland Duncan - HG 24
Charles English - S 25
Forster family - C 46, 53
Von Glehn family - S 25
W G Grace - S 40
Sir George Grove - S 8, 26
Robert Harrild - S 25, 69, 75-76
Horniman family - FH 19, 19A
Ephraim & John How - C 44, 47
Lady Hunloke - S 44
Richard Jefferies - S 70
Lawrie family - S 27, 37
Henry Littleton - S 27
Sir George Livesey - S 16
Margaret & Rachel McMillan - HG 14
August Manns - S 77D
Eleanor Marx - S 27
Edith Nesbit - GP 4
Professor Richard Owen - CP 16
Sir Joseph Paxton - CP 4, 8, 24
Camille Pissarro - S 35, 55; CP 20A
Thomas Rammell - CP 13
Dame Cecily Saunders - S 41
Sir Ernest Shackleton - S 26
Tetley family - FH 40
John Thackeray - C 11
Thomas Tilling - C 35, 52
David Ximenes - S 27

Public buildings (present & former)
Forest Hill Fire Station - FH 43
Forest Hill Library - FH 22
Forest Hill Swimming Baths - FH 22
Grove Park Hospital - GP 5
Hither Green Hospital - HG 15
Laurence House - C 24A
Louise House - FH 22
Old Bath House - S 10

Rivers Depot - C 22
St Christophers Hospice - S 41
Sydenham Library - S 9
Sydenham Public Lecture Hall - S 77B
Torridon Library - HG 21

Pubs
Baring Hall - GP 2
Bell - S 10
Bird in Hand - FH 20
Black Horse & Harrow - C 15
Blythe Hill Tavern - C 29
Bricklayers Arms - S 73
Cambridge - CP 20B
Chandos - FH 38
Dartmouth - HG 16-17
Dartmouth Arms - FH 20
Downham Tavern - C 54A
Duke of Edinburgh - S 48
Dulwich Wood House - S 58
Fellowship - C 50A
Fewterer & Firkin (Greyhound) - S 23
Foresters Arms - FH 51
Fox & Hounds - S 77C
George - C 12
Golden Lion - S 5
Goose & Granite (Rising Sun) - C 8
Green Man - C 45
Hobgoblin (Railway Signal) - FH 28
Paxton Arms - CP 18
Plough & Harrow - C 9
Prince Alfred - S 7
Queens Arms - HG 4
Railway Tavern - S 12A
Railway Telegraph - FH 22
Rutland Arms - C 36
Sir John Morden - HG 5
Sportsman - CP 20C
Spotted Cow - HG 7
Station - HG 2
Talma - S 48
Tigers Head - C 47
White Swan - CP 20A
Woodman - S 77C

Schools, colleges etc
Crofton School - C 4
Ennersdale School - HG 3
Fairlawn School - FH 10
Forest Hill School - FH 46
Haseltine School - S 11
Hither Green School - HG 11
Holbeach School - C 5
Holy Trinity School - S 73
Horniman School - FH 16
Kelvin Grove School - S 77B
New Woodlands School - S 77B
Priory House School - C 20
Rathfern School - C 38
St Dunstans College - C 27

96 - INDEX

St Francisca Cabrini School - FH 5
St Michaels School - S 18
Sydenham High School - S 33
Sydenham School - S 74
Torridon School - HG 23

Streets
Albion Villas Road - S 72
Amberley Grove - S 33
Anerley Hill - CP 18-20
Ardgowan Road - HG 19
Baring Road - GP 2-4
Bell Green - S 10, 14-17
Blythe Hill Lane - C 30
Border Road - S 38
Brockley Park - FH 34-36
Bromley Road - C 18-21, 45-47, 52
Brownhill Road - C 16; HG 19-20
Campshill Road - HG 5-6
Catford Broadway - C 25
Catford Hill - C 39-40
Catford Road - C 1-2, 23-25
Champion Road - S 18
Charlecote Grove - S 77B
Charleville Circus - S 32
Cheseman Street - S 73
Church Road - CP 20B
Clyde Place - FH 21
College Road - S 57-58
Coombe Road - S 48
Cox's Walk - S 55-56
Crescent Wood Road - S 57-59
Crystal Palace Parade - CP 4, 21
Crystal Palace Park Road - CP 25
Dartmouth Road - S 73-74; FH 20-22
Dacres Road - FH 48-49
Davids Road - FH 29
Devonshire Road - FH 28, 30-31
Downham Way - C 54-56
Eliot Bank - S 77A
Elm Lane - C 37
Farquhar Road - CP 21
Fordel Road - HG 19
George Lane - C 12; HG 14
Hafton Road - HG 19
Halifax Street - S 77C
Hall Drive - S 37
Hindsleys Place - FH 51
Hither Green Lane - HG 7-10, 12-13, 19
Holbeach Road - C 5-6
Honor Oak Park - FH 1-5
Honor Oak Rise - FH 6
Honor Oak Road - FH 10-15, 17-18
Horniman Drive - FH 12, 16
Jew's Walk - S 27, 77D
Kelvin Grove - S 77B
Kirkdale - S 23-24, 67, 77
Laleham Road - HG 17
Lawrie Park Avenue - S 35
Lawrie Park Gardens - S 34

Lawrie Park Road - S 40
Leahurst Road - HG 3
Liphook Crescent -FH 12C
London Road - FH 24-26
Longton Avenue - S 28
Longton Grove - S 28A
Low Cross Wood Lane - S 60
Lowther Hill - FH 35, 37
Malham Road - FH 33
Manor Mount - FH 17
Marvels Lane - GP 5-6
Mayow Road - FH 45-46
Montacute Road - C 26
Monument Gardens - HG 6
Mount Ash Road - S 77B
Mount Gardens - S 77A
Northover - C 59
Ormanton Road - S 28B
Panmure Road - S 77B
Peak Hill - S 66
Peak Hill Avenue - S 65
Perry Hill - C 35-36
Perry Vale - FH 42-43, 50-51
Redberry Grove - S 71
Redfern Road - HG 18
Round Hill - S 73E, 75
Ravensbourne Park - C 26
Ravensbourne Park Crescent - C 26
Rushey Green - C 7-15
Rutland Park - C 36
Rutland Walk - C 36
St Fillans Road - HG 19
Sangley Road - C 17
South Road - FH 40-41
Springbank Road - HG 1
Stanstead Road - FH 32; C 28-29, 32
Staplehurst Road - HG 2
Stondon Rise - FH 39
Sydenham Avenue - S 36
Sydenham Hill - S 43-44, 48-54, 57-58, 63-64
Sydenham Park - S 68-69
Sydenham Park Road - S 70
Sydenham Road - S 4-9, 19, 22
Taylors Lane - S 49
Taymount Rise - FH 26-27
Thicket Road - CP 27
Torridon Road - HG 21-23
Venner Road - S 2
Vineyard Close - C 40
Waldegrave Road - CP 28
Watlington Grove - S 7
Wellmeadow Road - HG 19
Wells Park Road - S 29A, 47
Westow Hill - CP 20A
Westwood Hill - S 25-26, 30-31, 33A, 40A, 42
Woolstone Road - C 34